Miriam B. Loo's

HOLIDAY COOKBOOK

Recipes Compiled by Miriam B. Loo

This book is dedicated to all the very special Current customers with whom I have had the privilege and pleasure of sharing recipes for over thirty years.

Photography by Skip Whitcomb and Pierre DeBernay
Illustrated by Marsha K. Howe

Dear Friends,

The holidays are a time for celebrating, and one of the most pleasant aspects of this is preparing special foods to share with the people you care about.

The **Holiday Cookbook** has been planned to make your holiday entertaining and gift-giving both easier and deliciously gratifying. Recipes have been selected for their luscious, "something extra" taste as well as their appropriateness to festive occasions. Besides individual recipes, four complete menus are included at the end of the book to help you provide the very happiest holiday gatherings for family and friends.

Food, whether served to guests or given as gifts, is one of the most basic and creative ways of saying "I care about you." It is my hope that this book will help to increase your own pleasures and the enjoyment of those close to you during this wonderful season.

And, because you, our Current customers, are special to me, I would truly enjoy and appreciate hearing your responses to this book, and what you would like to see in future cookbooks from Current in the years to come. Please address any comments you may have to me, in care of the Current Kitchen, Current, Inc., Colorado Springs, Colorado 80941. Thank you.

Happy Holidays!

Miriam B. Loo

Miriam B. Loo

CONTENTS

APPETIZERS

THREE FILLING CIRCLE SANDWICH

2 ½-inch crosswise slices Herb Casserole Bread (see page 72*)

First filling:
1 8-ounce package cream cheese, softened

2 tablespoons dairy sour cream
2 ounces blue cheese, crumbled
¼ cup real mayonnaise

Second filling:
2 4½-ounce cans deviled ham
2 teaspoons Dijon-style mustard

4 teaspoons sweet pickle relish
2 teaspoons cream-style horseradish

Third filling:
3 hard-cooked eggs, minced
1½ tablespoons real mayonnaise

¼ teaspoon salt
¼ teaspoon dried dill weed

Garnish:
1 small cucumber
2 ounces small Alaskan shrimp shelled, cleaned and cooked

Pitted ripe olives
Pimiento-stuffed green olives
Cocktail tomatoes

In small bowl, mix together cream cheese, sour cream, blue cheese and mayonnaise. Spread both slices with mixture. Mix together deviled ham, mustard, pickle relish and horseradish; spread in large circle in center of each slice of bread to within 1½ inches of edge. Combine minced egg with mayonnaise, salt and dill weed; spoon into smaller circle in center of ham and smooth with spatula. Place one slice of filled bread on top of other (filling side up), pressing lightly. On top layer, complete garnish with thin slices of cucumber in large outer circle. Accent with tiny shrimp, slices of olives and cocktail tomatoes in an eye-appealing design.

*Note: A bakery round loaf may be used in place of Herb Casserole Bread.

Makes 8 to 10 wedge-shaped servings

7

CRAB QUICHE

"This recipe brings a whole new meaning to quiche. Rich and flavorful, it would make a nice entrée for a ladies' luncheon, as well as an appetizer."

Pastry:

1½ cups all-purpose flour	½ cup solid vegetable shortening
½ teaspoon salt	4 to 5 tablespoons cold water

Sift together flour and salt; cut in shortening until pieces are size of small peas. Sprinkle with cold water, 1 tablespoon at a time, while mixing with fork, until completely moist. Form into balls; flatten on lightly floured surface. Place in foil and refrigerate for 1 hour or overnight. Roll on lightly floured surface to ⅛-inch thick and fit into 9-inch pie plate. Make rim around edge.

Filling:

1 cup shredded natural Swiss cheese	1½ cups half-and-half
1 7½-ounce can crab meat, drained, flaked, cartilage removed	½ teaspoon salt
	½ teaspoon grated lemon rind
3 scallions, thinly sliced with 1 inch of greens	1 teaspoon fresh lemon juice
	¼ teaspoon dry mustard
4 eggs, beaten	¼ teaspoon ground mace
	¼ cup sliced, toasted almonds

Arrange cheese evenly over bottom of pastry shell. Top with crab meat; sprinkle with scallions. Combine eggs, half-and-half, salt, lemon rind and juice, dry mustard and mace. Pour over crab meat. Top with sliced almonds. Bake in a preheated 325°F oven for about 45 minutes or until set. Remove from oven and let stand 10 minutes before serving.

Serves 6

CREAM OF MUSHROOM SOUP

"So smooth; rich with cream and the light flavor of mushrooms."

1 pound fresh mushrooms	2 cups heavy cream
4 cups chicken broth (your own or canned)	2 tablespoons dry sherry *or* cognac
	1½ teaspoons salt
2 tablespoons butter *or* margarine	¼ teaspoon Tabasco® pepper sauce
3 tablespoons all-purpose flour	

Remove stems from clean mushrooms. Chop stems and add to chicken broth in large saucepan. Simmer for 45 minutes. Strain; discard stems. Mix butter or margarine and flour to paste; roll into tiny balls. Bring broth to boil; drop in balls and beat with whisk until absorbed and sauce is slightly thickened. Slice mushroom caps and add to broth; simmer 10 minutes. Heat cream in saucepan; add sherry or cognac. Add cream mixture to broth mixture; season with salt and Tabasco® pepper sauce. Heat until just hot and serve in heated bowls.

Serves 8

CHEESE TARTLETS

"This is a good do-ahead. Wrap in foil when cold. Reheat in low oven . . ."

Pastry:
1⅔ cups all-purpose flour	1 egg yolk
¼ teaspoon salt	¼ cup cold water
½ cup real butter, chilled	1 tablespoon vegetable oil

Place flour and salt into mixing bowl. Cut chilled butter in pea-size bits into flour and work mixture until texture of oatmeal. (Pastry can also be made in food processor.) Beat egg yolk with cold water and oil. Make a well in center of flour-butter mixture and pour in egg. Mix with fork and press dough into ball. Wrap well and refrigerate for 1 hour. Roll on lightly floured surface to ⅛-inch thick; fit into a 10-inch pie plate or a 24-cup (1½-inch each) muffin pan. Prick well with fork and refrigerate.

Cheese filling:
1 cup finely diced natural Swiss cheese	1 cup heavy cream
	Salt and freshly ground pepper
2 eggs	¼ teaspoon ground nutmeg
	¾ cup grated natural Swiss cheese

Sprinkle a bit of Swiss cheese in uncooked shell, pressing cheese lightly into pastry. Refrigerate. Beat eggs, cream, salt, pepper and nutmeg together. Fill chilled shells and sprinkle with remaining grated Swiss cheese. Bake small shells in a preheated 400°F oven for 12 to 15 minutes or until puffed up and golden. For 10-inch shell, bake in a preheated 400°F oven for 25 to 30 minutes or until puffed and golden. Remove from oven and serve slightly warm.

Makes 1 10-inch tart or 24 individual tarts

SAVORY CHEESE STUFFED MUSHROOMS

36 medium-size fresh mushrooms, washed
3 tablespoons butter *or* margarine
¼ cup minced green pepper
2 tablespoons minced pimiento
¼ cup minced onion
1½ cups soft bread crumbs (about 3 slices)
¾ cup shredded Monterey Jack cheese
½ teaspoon salt
½ teaspoon dried thyme, crushed
¼ teaspoon ground turmeric
¼ teaspoon freshly ground pepper
1 tablespoon butter *or* margarine

Remove stems from mushrooms and mince enough to measure ⅓ cup. Melt 3 tablespoons butter or margarine in skillet; add chopped mushroom stems, green pepper, pimiento and onion. Cook and stir until tender, about 5 to 7 minutes. Remove from heat; stir in remaining ingredients except mushroom caps and 1 tablespoon butter or margarine. Melt remaining 1 tablespoon butter or margarine in a shallow baking pan. Fill mushroom caps with stuffing mixture; place in pan. Bake in a preheated 350°F oven for 15 to 20 minutes or until lightly browned.

Serves 8 to 10

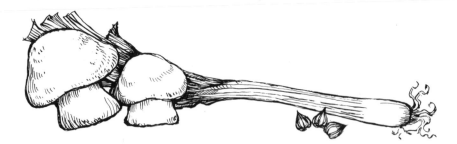

ITALIAN STUFFED MUSHROOMS

24 medium-large fresh mushrooms
2 tablespoons olive oil
¼ cup minced scallions *or* onion
1 clove garlic, minced
¼ cup minced green pepper
1 tablespoon minced fresh parsley
½ teaspoon salt
¼ teaspoon freshly ground pepper
¼ teaspoon Italian seasoning
3 tablespoons grated Parmesan cheese
3 tablespoons minced capers
1 tablespoon fine bread crumbs
1 egg yolk + 1 teaspoon water

Wash, dry and stem mushrooms. Mince stems. Heat olive oil in skillet; add mushroom stems, scallions or onion, garlic and green pepper. Sauté, stirring for 5 minutes. Mix in parsley, salt, pepper, Italian seasoning, cheese, capers and bread crumbs. Remove from heat. Beat egg yolk with 1 teaspoon water and add to stuffing, mixing well. Stuff mushrooms, place on oiled baking sheet and bake in a preheated 375°F oven for 15 minutes.

Serves 6 to 8

ONION STUFFED MUSHROOMS

24 small fresh mushrooms
¼ cup minced onion
¼ cup grated Parmesan cheese
½ teaspoon salt

¼ teaspoon freshly ground pepper
¼ teaspoon paprika
3 tablespoons olive oil

Wash, dry and stem mushrooms. Chop stems and combine with onion, cheese, salt, pepper and paprika. Add 1 tablespoon olive oil to this mixture and stuff mushrooms. Place remaining 2 tablespoons olive oil in baking dish and spread. Heat pan in a preheated 375°F oven; arrange mushrooms in pan. Bake 10 minutes. Serve on toast rounds or with cocktail forks.

Serves 6 to 8

SAVORY CHEESE STUFFED MUSHROOMS (left) — "Warm up your guests' appetite with this mushroom overture."

ITALIAN STUFFED MUSHROOMS (center) — "A vegetable mixture stuffing, accented with Italian seasoning."

ONION STUFFED MUSHROOMS (right) — "Quick, simple, tasty."

COLD FISH MOUSSE WITH SALSA VERDE

"This recipe will make a fish lover out of even the most finicky eater . . ."

1 1-pound package frozen flounder or sole, defrosted	⅛ teaspoon grated nutmeg
2 eggs	½ teaspoon fresh lemon juice
1¼ teaspoons salt	Pinch of cayenne pepper
Freshly ground white pepper to taste	1½ cups heavy cream
	Minced fresh parsley for garnish

Preheat oven to 350°F. Generously butter a 5-cup mold. Cut fish into 1½-inch cubes and place in a bowl of food processor or blender. Add eggs, salt, pepper, nutmeg, lemon juice and cayenne. Blend until coarsely chopped in on/off spurts. Gradually add cream while continuing to blend. When fluffy and light, pour mousse into buttered mold. Smooth over top and cover with round of buttered wax paper cut to fit. Place mold in a shallow pan 2 to 3 inches larger in diameter; add boiling water to depth of 1 inch. Return water to boil on stove top; place in oven (do not allow water to boil while in oven, simmer only) and bake mousse until set, approximately 45 minutes. Let stand until cooled; chill. Unmold onto a serving dish and serve with Salsa Verde.

Note: Spoon a ribbon of Salsa Verde down the middle of mousse and sprinkle with minced parsley before serving. Or make individual servings by placing a slice of mousse on a lettuce leaf, nap with sauce and sprinkle with parsley.

Serves 6 to 8

SALSA VERDE

½ of a 10½-ounce package frozen chopped spinach, thawed	1 tablespoon fresh lemon juice
1 egg	2 tablespoons minced scallions
½ teaspoon dry mustard	2 tablespoons minced fresh parsley
½ teaspoon salt	½ teaspoon dried dill weed
	½ cup vegetable oil

Put all ingredients except oil in blender or food processor; purée. Slowly add oil while machine is running. Taste for additional seasoning. Serve warm or chilled over the mousse.

Note: This sauce is also delicious with cold meats or heated and served over pasta.

Serves 6 to 8

CRAB AND SWEET CORN SOUP

"This is a prize-winning soup. Served in a large bowl, it would be good for a Sunday evening supper . . ."

2 slices green ginger root, ¼-inch thick
1 chicken bouillon cube
1½ quarts chicken broth (your own or canned)
2 cups fresh, canned or frozen sweet corn
1 cup crab meat, drained, flaked, cartilage removed

2 tablespoons cornstarch
2 tablespoons dry sherry
Salt and freshly ground pepper to taste
2 tablespoons thinly shredded, boiled ham
2 tablespoons minced fresh chives

Add slices of ginger root and chicken bouillon cube to broth in large saucepan. Bring to boil; simmer 10 minutes. Chop corn in blender or food processor. Add corn to broth, bring to boil and simmer 10 minutes. Add crab, cornstarch dissolved in sherry and simmer, stirring until thickened, about 10 minutes. Season with salt and pepper to taste. Remove ginger root. Serve in individual hot bowls and sprinkle with ham and chives.

Serves 8

ESCARGOTS IN BUTTER SAUCE

"Snails being as expensive as they are, this will be for a super special occasion — easy to prepare and delicious! If you have shells, this recipe can be used to stuff them . . ."

1 cup real butter, softened
2 tablespoons minced shallots
2 tablespoons minced garlic
2 tablespoons dry vermouth
1 tablespoon Worcestershire sauce
1 tablespoon minced fresh parsley

1 teaspoon brandy
1 teaspoon fresh lemon juice
½ teaspoon salt
4 grinds fresh pepper
3 dozen large snails

Mix all ingredients except snails and heat in large skillet. Add snails and simmer over low heat 10 to 15 minutes. Serve in a chafing dish with cocktail forks and slices of crusty French bread.

Serves 4 to 6

SHRIMP IN PORT CREAM

¼ cup butter *or* margarine
8 scallions, chopped
1 pound small Alaskan shrimp,
    shelled, cleaned and cooked
¼ cup dry port wine

4 egg yolks
1 cup heavy cream
½ cup coarsely chopped fresh
    parsley
Salt and freshly ground pepper

Preheat oven to 325°F. Melt butter or margarine in large skillet. Add scallions and sauté 5 minutes. Add shrimp, mix carefully into butter or margarine mixture; add port and simmer 3 minutes. Transfer shrimp to a well-greased, shallow, 9-inch round ovenproof pan or 6 ramekin dishes. In bowl, beat together yolks and cream. Add parsley; season with salt and pepper. Pour custard mixture over shrimp. Bake until set, about 35 minutes.

Note: If making a single tart, let cool 10 minutes before cutting into serving wedges.

Serves 6

SHRIMP IN PORT CREAM — *"This tasty shrimp and port combination (shown here in ramekin dishes) is surprisingly easy to make and such a crowd pleaser."*
SHELLFISH APPETIZER — *"Start your dinner with a taste of the sea in a rich sauce served in individual shell containers."*

SHELLFISH APPETIZER

¼ cup butter *or* margarine
¼ cup minced shallots *or* scallions
1 pound medium shrimp, cooked, shelled, deveined and cut in half lengthwise

½ pound prepared crab meat, frozen *or* canned
Salt and freshly ground white pepper to taste
1 tablespoon dry vermouth

In saucepan, melt butter or margarine; add shallots or scallions and sauté, stirring for 5 minutes. Stir in shrimp and crab; sprinkle with salt and pepper to taste. Add 1 tablespoon vermouth; stir over high heat for 1 minute. Remove from heat.

Sauce:
2 tablespoons cornstarch
2 cups heavy cream
1 teaspoon tomato paste
2 tablespoons dry vermouth
Salt and freshly ground white pepper to taste

2 teaspoons fresh lemon juice
⅓ cup grated Parmesan cheese
⅓ cup finely crushed rich cracker crumbs
2 tablespoons real butter, melted

For sauce: In bowl, mix cornstarch, cream and tomato paste. Mix until smooth; add to seafood mixture with 2 tablespoons vermouth. Return to heat and cook, stirring, for 4 to 5 minutes or until sauce thickens. Taste for salt and pepper; add lemon juice. Spoon shellfish mixture into greased individual shell containers. Sprinkle with a mixture of Parmesan cheese, cracker crumbs and butter. Shells can be refrigerated at this point until just before serving. Arrange shells on baking sheet and put in a preheated 400°F oven for 15 minutes or until hot and bubbly. Do not overcook.

Serves 8

OLD-FASHIONED TOMATO SOUP

"A beautiful sight to behold; creamy red tomato soup in contrast with avocado green."

2 tablespoons butter *or* margarine
1 teaspoon minced onion
3 tablespoons all-purpose flour
2 cups milk
¾ teaspoon salt

¼ teaspoon freshly ground pepper
4 cups tomato juice, heated
⅛ teaspoon baking soda
½ bay leaf (optional)
1 ripe avocado

Melt butter or margarine in saucepan over medium-high heat and add onion; sauté 5 minutes. Add flour; stir for 5 minutes. Pour in milk; add salt and pepper. Use whisk to blend well and simmer for 5 minutes. Meanwhile, heat tomato juice to boiling, add soda, then add to cream sauce mixture. Add bay leaf and continue to simmer for 10 minutes, stirring occasionally. Remove bay leaf. Serve in hot bowls with 2 thin slices of ripe avocado floating on top of each.

Serves 6 to 8

SPINACH TART APPETIZER — "A nutritious, colorful opening to any meal."

SPINACH TART APPETIZER

2 10½-ounce packages frozen
  chopped spinach
2 tablespoons minced shallots *or*
  scallions
¼ cup butter *or* margarine
¼ cup minced ham
Salt and freshly ground pepper to
  taste
Sprinkling of grated nutmeg

3 whole eggs
½ cup dairy sour cream
1½ cups half-and-half
½ cup + 1 tablespoon grated
  Parmesan cheese
1 medium tomato, peeled, cut into
  thin wedges
Minced fresh parsley for garnish

Thaw spinach and drain well. Sauté shallots or scallions in butter or margarine 2 to 3 minutes. Add spinach and sauté over high heat, stirring constantly until liquid has evaporated and spinach is dry. Place spinach in bowl with ham, seasonings, eggs, sour cream, half-and-half and ½ cup Parmesan cheese and lightly blend. Process in blender or food processor in 3 batches until puréed. Prepare a 10-inch pie plate by greasing and sprinkling with remaining 1 tablespoon Parmesan cheese. Spoon in spinach mixture. Bake in preheated 350°F oven for 25 to 30 minutes or until set. Remove from oven; place thin wedges of tomatoes in circle on top. Dust lightly with salt, pepper and minced parsley. Return to oven for 5 minutes to heat through. Remove from oven; cool 10 minutes before slicing into serving wedges.

Serves 6 to 8

ENTRÉES

CROWN ROAST OF PORK

"A royal presentation of succulent pork . . ."

1 16-rib Crown Roast of Pork (have
   butcher prepare in crown form)

Salt and freshly ground pepper
1 teaspoon dried rosemary

Garnish:
Cinnamon Apple Salad (see page 49)

Preheat oven to 450°F. Carefully rub roast with salt, pepper and rosemary. Wrap a piece of foil around ends of bones to keep from burning. Put roast in oven and reduce heat to 350°F, allowing cooking time of 20 to 25 minutes per pound or about 3 hours. If using a meat thermometer, it should register 170°F. One hour before roast is done, remove from oven and fill cavity with the following Apple and Onion Dressing. Return roast to oven and complete cooking. Remove meat to serving platter and garnish with Cinnamon-Apple Salad. Put paper frills on rib bone tips. (These may be obtained from butcher or specialty shop.)

Note: A boned, rolled loin of pork may be used in place of the Crown Roast.

Serves 10 to 12 (allowing 2 chops for larger helpings)

APPLE AND ONION DRESSING

1 cup butter *or* margarine
1 cup chopped onion
2 cups peeled, cored and diced
   apples
1 cup chopped celery
6 cups diced fresh bread, oven dried
¼ cup dry sherry

1½ cups raisins, currants *or* golden
   raisins *or* ½ cup each
½ teaspoon salt
1 teaspoon paprika
2 tablespoons fresh lemon juice
¼ cup chicken broth (your own *or*
   canned)

In a large skillet, melt butter or margarine; add onion, apples and celery and sauté for 7 minutes. Add all remaining ingredients except chicken broth; toss lightly. Remove from heat and stuff Crown Roast. Put remainder of dressing in small greased casserole; add chicken broth and bake, covered, beside roast. If cooking rolled loin, all dressing should be put in casserole and chicken broth increased to ½ cup. Cover and bake for 1 hour in 350°F oven.

Serves 10 to 12

ROAST TURKEY

"Use this method or your own favorite recipe . . ."

1 turkey for roasting, fresh or frozen
(If frozen, use package directions
to thaw)
Butter *or* margarine, softened

Salt and freshly ground pepper
3 cups hot turkey broth (made from
giblets and neck)
½ cup butter *or* margarine, melted

Pat thawed bird dry with paper towels. Rub skin areas liberally with softened butter or margarine, salt and pepper. Loosely place stuffing in neck and body cavity. Close openings with skewers and foil and use string where needed. Preheat oven to 450°F. Place bird directly into oven and reduce heat to 325°F. After first ½ hour of cooking, baste bird frequently with pan drippings and mixture of turkey broth and butter or margarine. Cook to an internal temperature of 180° to 185°F. The center of stuffing should reach at least 165°F. If not using thermometer, allow 20 to 25 minutes per pound for birds up to 6 pounds; 15 to 20 minutes per pound for birds weighing up to 16 pounds, and 13 to 15 minutes per pound for larger turkeys. After removing from oven, let sit for 20 minutes in warm place before carving.

Note: Allow ¾ to 1 pound per person to be served.

DRESSING FOR TURKEY

"Allow about ¾ cup per pound of bird for each serving, dressed weight . . ."

½ cup butter *or* margarine
1 cup chopped onion
2 cups cleaned and sliced fresh
mushrooms
1 cup chopped celery
½ cup chopped fresh parsley
2 teaspoons dried basil, crushed
1 teaspoon dried, rubbed sage

1½ teaspoons salt
1 teaspoon paprika
¼ teaspoon ground nutmeg
8 cups crustless day-old *or* slightly
toasted, diced white, whole wheat
or corn bread crumbs
½ cup milk *or* stock
4 eggs, lightly beaten

In skillet, melt butter or margarine and sauté chopped onion and sliced mushrooms. Add celery and sauté for 5 to 7 minutes; add parsley, basil, sage, salt, paprika and nutmeg. Mix this into bread cubes or cornbread crumbs. Add milk or stock to beaten eggs and mix into stuffing. Add additional moisture if needed. Taste for seasoning.

Makes about 10 cups dressing

HOT FISH MOUSSE WITH SAUCE DUGLÉRÉ

Follow directions for Cold Fish Mousse (page 12). After baking approximately 45 minutes, let stand 10 minutes in a warm place. Unmold onto a hot serving dish. Pour a ribbon of Sauce Dugléré (following recipe) down the center and sprinkle with minced parsley. Serve rest of sauce separately.

SAUCE DUGLÉRÉ
(Tomato and Cream Sauce)

"A velvety sauce, so delicate in flavor."

1 tablespoon butter *or* margarine
3 tablespoons minced onion
1 tablespoon minced scallions
⅓ cup dry vermouth
2 cups peeled, seeded and chopped tomatoes

Salt and freshly ground pepper to taste
1 cup heavy cream
⅛ teaspoon anise-flavored extract *or* ¼ teaspoon anise seeds (optional)

Melt butter or margarine in saucepan; add onion and scallions. Cook, stirring, until wilted. Add vermouth and simmer 5 minutes. Add tomatoes, salt and pepper; simmer 10 minutes. Add cream, stirring occasionally; cook over moderate heat until thickened, about 10 to 15 minutes. Add anise-flavored extract or anise seeds (optional). Serve this sauce hot with the Hot Fish Mousse.

Serves 6 to 8

VENISON OR ELK ROAST

"I have served this to people who claim they don't like game, but thought this was great . . ."

4 to 6 pound deer *or* elk roast
⅓ cup all-purpose flour, seasoned with salt and freshly ground pepper
3 tablespoons bacon fat
1 8-ounce can tomato sauce
1 cup Burgundy wine

½ cup minced onion
½ cup chopped celery
¼ cup chopped fresh parsley
2 carrots, coarsely chopped
2 4-ounce cans mushrooms, drained
2 tablespoons dried oregano

Remove fat and bone from meat. Rinse, dry and tie into shape. Dredge roast in flour mixture. Heat bacon fat in heavy covered roaster; add meat and brown slowly on all sides. Add all other ingredients and bring to boil. Cover and place in a preheated 325°F oven for about 4 hours or until meat is tender. Turn roast from time to time. Serve sauce separately.

Note: Use less oregano if you are sure your meat is not real gamey.

Serves 6

CRANBERRY PORK CHOPS

6 pork chops, 1-inch thick
½ cup all-purpose flour, seasoned
with salt and freshly ground
pepper
2 tablespoons vegetable oil
2 cups fresh cranberries, washed and
picked over

¾ cup water
¾ cup sugar
½ cup honey
¼ teaspoon ground cloves
¼ teaspoon ground nutmeg
¼ teaspoon ground cinnamon

Dredge chops in flour mixture; brown in vegetable oil in skillet. Mix cranberries with remaining ingredients. Place chops in a shallow baking dish in a single layer; top with cranberry mixture. Cover and bake in a preheated 350°F oven for 30 minutes, remove cover and bake for an additional 30 minutes.

Serves 6

CRANBERRY PORK CHOPS —
"Another autumn fruit accompaniment
that turns pork into a real holiday entrée."

SALMON BAKED IN FOIL

"The natural goodness of salmon is enhanced with the lemony butter flavor . . ."

1 3 to 4 pound whole fresh salmon
1 lemon, thinly sliced, seeds removed
¼ cup dry vermouth
¼ teaspoon salt
Several drops Tabasco® pepper sauce
½ cup real butter, melted
Lemon, ripe olives and fresh parsley for garnish

Wash and pat fish dry. Prepare a piece of heavy duty foil large enough to completely wrap fish loosely. Place foil on jelly roll pan or similar container; grease foil. Place 3 to 4 slices of lemon in center of foil; place fish on top. Add vermouth, salt and Tabasco® pepper sauce to melted butter. Brush inside of fish cavity with butter mixture and add 2 or 3 slices of lemon. Bring up edges of foil around fish. Pour remaining butter mixture over fish; place remaining lemon slices on top of fish.

Loosely bring edges of foil over top of fish and fold over 2 times to form tight seal. Preheat oven to 350°F and bake 15 minutes per pound. Do not overcook.

Last 10 minutes of cooking time check with a probe in thickest part of fish. It should be flaky. To serve, carefully remove skin and dark fatty parts of fish on upper side. Place fish on heated platter and garnish with fresh lemon and ripe olive slices; surround with sprigs of fresh parsley. Serve the lemon butter sauce separately or use the following Easy Hollandaise Sauce.

Serves 10 to 12

EASY HOLLANDAISE SAUCE

1 cup dairy sour cream
1 cup real mayonnaise
2 teaspoons Dijon-style mustard
1 tablespoon fresh lemon juice

Combine all ingredients in small saucepan; cook, stirring, over low heat until heated through. May be kept hot using double boiler.

Makes 2 cups sauce

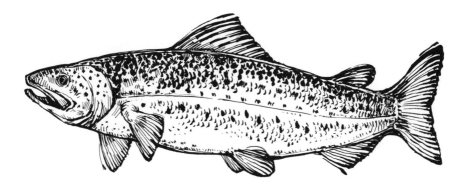

HAM-SPINACH ROLL WITH TARRAGON-WINE SAUCE

"A good recipe for a ladies' luncheon."

Spinach Roll:

⅔ cup dried, finely crushed bread crumbs

3 10½-ounce packages chopped frozen spinach

½ cup butter *or* margarine, melted

1 teaspoon salt

¼ teaspoon freshly ground pepper

¼ to ½ teaspoon ground nutmeg

5 eggs, separated

¼ teaspoon cream of tartar

¼ cup grated Parmesan cheese

For spinach roll: Grease a 10x15-inch jelly roll pan; line with wax paper. Grease paper and sprinkle lightly with fine dried bread crumbs. Cook spinach according to package directions and drain well, removing as much moisture as possible. In bowl, combine spinach with butter or margarine; stir in salt, pepper and nutmeg. Beat egg yolks until light and lemon colored; fold into spinach. Beat egg whites with ¼ teaspoon cream of tartar until stiff but not dry peaks. Fold into spinach mixture; spread evenly in jelly roll pan. Sprinkle lightly with Parmesan cheese. Bake in a preheated 350°F oven for 15 to 18 minutes or until firm. Invert onto a greased piece of foil slightly larger than pan. Carefully remove wax paper from spinach. Prepare the following wine sauce.

Wine Sauce:

1 cup dry white wine

½ cup minced onion

1 tablespoon dried tarragon

1 cup chicken broth (your own *or* canned)

2 tablespoons cornstarch

¼ cup tomato paste

¾ cup half-and-half

2 cups cooked diced ham

Chopped fresh parsley

For wine sauce: Combine wine with onion and tarragon in saucepan; bring to boil, cover and simmer 15 minutes. Add 4 tablespoons chicken broth to cornstarch; blend well and add remaining chicken broth. Add to wine mixture; stir in tomato paste. Cook over medium heat, stirring until thickened. Add half-and-half slowly while stirring to blend well. Do not boil. Add diced ham. Spread half of wine sauce onto the baked spinach. With the aid of foil, roll baked spinach up lengthwise and onto a serving platter. Spoon remaining wine sauce over roll and garnish with a little chopped parsley.

Note: The wine sauce without the ham is good to use on baked ham, fish, chicken or green vegetables.

Serves 6 to 8

MUSHROOM AND SAUSAGE PIE

"A luncheon or supper favorite served with a green salad and the Ginger-Pumpkin Dessert (page 79) for dessert."

1 9-inch unbaked pastry shell	½ cup minced fresh parsley
1 pound bulk pork sausage, medium spiced	2 eggs
	1 cup half-and-half
1 pound small, whole fresh mushrooms, cleaned	½ cup grated Parmesan cheese
	¼ teaspoon salt

Crumble sausage in large skillet and add mushrooms. Cook over high heat, stirring frequently, until mushrooms and meat are lightly browned and all liquid from mushrooms has evaporated. Drain off any excess grease. Stir in parsley. Beat eggs with half-and-half and Parmesan cheese; blend in mushroom mixture and salt. Pour into unbaked pastry shell. Arrange mushrooms so that any stems are turned down in liquid. Bake in a preheated 400°F oven for 25 to 30 minutes, or until crust is well browned and filling is set. Let pie stand about 10 minutes before cutting.

Serves 6 to 8

PHEASANT IN CREAM

"An easy and delicious way to prepare this prized bird."

2 pheasants cut for frying *or* 3 whole breasts	¼ cup cognac *or* brandy
	2 cups heavy cream
3 tablespoons butter *or* margarine	1 cup dairy sour cream
Salt and freshly ground pepper	1 tablespoon all-purpose flour

Remove skin, bone pieces of meat. Melt butter or margarine in skillet and brown pheasant; sprinkle with salt and pepper to taste. In a small saucepan, warm cognac or brandy and pour into skillet. Light with match and shake pan; spoon juices over meat. Add heavy cream and cover. Simmer on stove top or place in a preheated 350°F oven; baste and turn frequently until tender — about 50 minutes to 1 hour. Remove meat from pan; keep warm. Add sour cream and flour mixed together. Simmer, stirring until sauce thickens. Check for salt and pepper and adjust if necessary. Return meat to skillet and heat through. Serve on heated platter garnished with sprigs of parsley if desired.

Note: If an herb flavor is desired, add 1½ teaspoons dried tarragon to heavy cream before adding to meat.

Serves 4 to 6

TURKEY OR CHICKEN VELOUTÉ

¼ cup chopped green pepper
1 tablespoon minced green onion
¼ cup + 2 tablespoons butter *or* margarine
2 tablespoons all-purpose flour
1 cup chicken broth (your own *or* canned)
2 cups half-and-half
3 egg yolks, beaten
3 cups cubed, cooked turkey *or* chicken

2 tablespoons chopped pimiento
1½ tablespoons fresh lemon juice
2 to 3 tablespoons dry sherry (optional)
1 cup thinly sliced, fresh mushrooms
¾ teaspoon salt *or* to taste
Freshly ground white pepper to taste
Patty shells *or* toast
Paprika
Fresh parsley sprigs

In a saucepan sauté green pepper and onion in butter or margarine until tender but not browned. Blend in flour and cook, stirring for 2 minutes. Slowly add broth and half-and-half. Cook, stirring constantly for a few minutes. Add some of the hot sauce to egg yolks, then add yolks to rest of sauce. Cook until thickened. Add turkey or chicken, pimiento, lemon juice, optional sherry and mushrooms. Stir together; add salt and white pepper to taste. Serve on patty shells or toast. Dust with paprika and garnish with a sprig of parsley.

Serves 8

PORK CHOPS VERACRUZ

"Simple and simply delicious."

¼ cup bacon fat
2 cloves garlic, minced
4 thick pork chops
2 teaspoons dry mustard
Salt and freshly ground pepper to taste

½ cup dry vermouth
¾ cup fresh orange juice
1 medium onion, thinly sliced
2 green peppers, cored, seeded, cut in strips

Heat bacon fat in skillet and sauté garlic without browning. Rub pork chops with mustard, salt and pepper. Brown in bacon fat. Add vermouth and orange juice; simmer 5 minutes uncovered. Layer onion and green pepper on chops. Cover skillet; simmer until meat is tender, about 40 minutes. Serve with rice.

Serves 4

TURKEY OR CHICKEN VELOUTÉ —
"A simple but elegant way to
use your leftover poultry."

CORNISH HENS WITH TARRAGON STUFFING

"Makes an elegant, but easy entrée . . ."

3 Cornish hens, cut in half

Tarragon stuffing:

2 tablespoons butter *or* margarine
3 shallots *or* scallions, minced
1 teaspoon dried tarragon leaves, crushed
⅓ cup chopped toasted almonds
1 tablespoon minced fresh parsley
3 cups soft bread crumbs
Salt and freshly ground pepper to taste

2 tablespoons chicken broth (your own or canned)
1 egg, lightly beaten
¼ cup butter *or* margarine, melted
Salt and freshly ground pepper to taste
1½ cups chicken broth (your own or canned)

To make tarragon stuffing: Melt 2 tablespoons butter or margarine in skillet; add shallots or scallions and sauté for 5 minutes. Add tarragon, almonds, parsley, bread crumbs and a sprinkle of salt and pepper. Mix well; remove from heat. Add 2 tablespoons chicken broth to lightly beaten egg; blend into hot mixture, stirring constantly. Oil shallow baking sheet large enough to hold hen halves; place 6 mounds of stuffing several inches apart. Brush each hen half with melted butter or margarine and sprinkle with salt and pepper. Place over mound of stuffing, pressing down a bit. Bake in a preheated 375°F oven for 45 minutes or until well-browned; baste occasionally with 1½ cups chicken broth mixed with remaining melted butter or margarine. When cooked, remove hens and stuffing with large spatula to serving dish.

Finishing sauce:

1 tablespoon butter *or* margarine, softened
1 tablespoon all-purpose flour

Salt and freshly ground pepper to taste
2 tablespoons brandy (optional)

For finishing sauce: Mix together butter or margarine with flour and set aside. Pour and scrape drippings from baking sheet into skillet; add any remaining basting sauce and bring to boil. Slowly add flour mixture to skillet, whisking to keep smooth. Simmer until thickened. Season with salt and pepper to taste. Add optional brandy, stirring a minute. Serve over Cornish hen halves.

Note: You can have your butcher cut the birds in half, even though they are frozen.

Serves 6

FLANK STEAK STROGANOFF

"A quick and tasty dish, yet inexpensive . . ."

2 pounds of flank steak
6 tablespoons butter *or* margarine
1 clove garlic, halved
1 cup chopped onion
½ pound fresh mushrooms, cleaned, and sliced
3 tablespoons all-purpose flour

Salt and freshly ground pepper to taste
3 beef bouillon cubes, crumbled
1 10½-ounce can beef broth
¼ cup dry vermouth
1½ teaspoons dried dill weed
1 cup dairy sour cream

Trim fat and gristle from meat. Place in freezer for ½ hour. Remove and with sharp knife cut steak in half lengthwise; cut each half in paper-thin slices. Heat 2 tablespoons butter or margarine in large skillet until very hot. Add ⅓ of the steak in one layer; brown quickly, stirring. Remove and continue until all steak is browned. Remove all steak. Add remaining butter or margarine to skillet; sauté garlic, onion and mushrooms, stirring over high heat for 5 minutes. Remove from heat and discard garlic. Stir in flour, salt and pepper; add bouillon cubes and stir in broth. Bring to boil, stirring until thickened. Reduce heat; add meat and simmer 15 minutes. Over low heat, stir in vermouth, dill and sour cream. Serve with rice or buttered noodles.

Serves 6 to 8

CHICKEN OR TURKEY HASH

"This would be tasty served on toasted cornbread; a scrumptious way to use leftover chicken or turkey . . ."

¼ cup butter *or* margarine
2 tablespoons all-purpose flour
1½ cups milk
1 egg yolk
⅓ pound pork sausage
½ cup chopped onion

2 cups diced cooked chicken *or* turkey
2 tablespoons minced fresh parsley
½ cup soft white bread crumbs
½ teaspoon grated lemon rind
Salt and freshly ground pepper to taste

Melt butter or margarine in saucepan; add flour and cook 2 to 3 minutes, stirring. Add milk and stir with whisk until thickened. Add a small amount of sauce to egg yolk and blend; return to remainder of sauce. Stir and set aside. In a skillet, cook sausage over medium heat, stirring until browned. Remove meat from skillet; cook onion in drippings until soft. Thoroughly drain fat from sausage and onion; discard drippings. Combine sausage, onion, chicken or turkey, parsley, bread crumbs and lemon rind with salt and pepper to taste. Add sauce and return to skillet to heat thoroughly.

Serves 4 to 6

FRUITED FLORENTINE POT ROAST

1 tablespoon butter *or* margarine
1 5-pound blade chuck roast
2 teaspoons garlic salt
½ cup brandy
1 1-pound 4-ounce can sliced
   pineapple
1 teaspoon beef stock base *or* 1
   bouillon cube

2 teaspoons fines herbes
10 large prunes, seeded
½ cup dried apricot halves
1 tablespoon cornstarch
2 tablespoons water
½ cup chopped green onions

Melt butter or margarine in Dutch oven. Brown roast well on both sides. Sprinkle with garlic salt during browning. Remove from heat. Add brandy and ignite, spooning liquid over roast until flame dies. Drain pineapple, reserving all syrup. Add syrup to roast along with beef stock base or bouillon cube. Sprinkle with fines herbes. Add prunes and apricots. Cover tightly and bake in a pre-heated 325°F oven for 2½ to 3 hours or until tender. Remove meat to platter and keep warm in oven. Remove fat from pan. Blend cornstarch into water and stir into pan juices until thickened. Add pineapple slices and green onions, spooning gravy over to heat through. Place fruits around meat and cover with sauce.

Serves 6

FRUITED FLORENTINE POT ROAST—
"A celebration of fruit and wine."

LAND AND SEA ON A BUN

"Simply delicious"

8 ounces diced turkey or chicken	2 teaspoons Dijon-style mustard
6½ ounces canned *or* frozen crab meat, drained and chopped	¼ teaspoon ground nutmeg
¼ cup chopped celery	6 buns
¼ cup real mayonnaise	12 slices bacon, cooked crisp and halved
2 tablespoons dry vermouth (optional)	6 slices natural Swiss cheese, halved

Combine turkey or chicken, crab meat, celery, mayonnaise, optional vermouth, mustard and nutmeg; mix well. Split buns. Top each half with turkey or chicken mixture, bacon slices and cheese. Broil 6 inches from heat until cheese melts, 3 to 5 minutes. Serve open-faced.

Note: With a bowl of soup and/or salad, this would make a delicious and nutritious supper or luncheon. Try bran muffins for a little different flavor.

Makes 6 sandwiches

VEGETABLES

YAM AND APPLE CASSEROLE

"A colorful combination of fruits and spices accents traditional holiday yams."

4 large yams
3 large cooking apples
3 tablespoons butter *or* margarine
1 tablespoon cornstarch
½ cup firmly packed brown sugar

1 tablespoon fresh lemon juice
2 cups apple juice, hot
½ teaspoon ground allspice
½ teaspoon ground cinnamon
½ cup raisins

Parboil the yams for 40 minutes; peel and slice ⅓-inch-thick. Peel, core and thinly slice apples. In small saucepan melt butter or margarine; add cornstarch and sugar. Mix in lemon juice, hot apple juice, allspice and cinnamon; continue to cook for 5 to 6 minutes. In a shallow greased casserole, alternate layers of sliced yams and apples. Sprinkle raisins over top. Pour over the hot apple juice mixture, cover with foil and bake in a preheated 375°F oven for 1 hour. Remove foil and continue baking for an additional 30 minutes, basting frequently.

Serves 10 to 12

SPINACH AND ONION MOLD

"A beautiful and different approach to serving spinach. Even the children will like it."

1 large head romaine lettuce
3 10½-ounce packages frozen
  chopped spinach
1 cup minced onion
6 tablespoons butter *or* margarine
¼ cup all-purpose flour
1 teaspoon salt
¼ teaspoon dried dill weed

1½ cups milk
5 eggs
½ cup cracker crumbs *or* 1 slice
  bread, crumbled
½ cup grated Parmesan cheese
Lemon slices, stuffed green olives *or*
  tomato roses

Grease 1½-quart baking dish. Drop 8 to 10 romaine leaves into boiling water until just wilted, about 1 minute. Arrange leaves, overlapping, in greased baking dish to line completely.

Cook spinach according to package directions; drain, press against sieve to remove moisture. Set aside. Sauté onions in butter or margarine until soft, stir in flour, salt and dill. Remove from heat. Stir in milk, return to heat and cook, stirring constantly until mixture thickens. Beat eggs in large bowl. Beat in hot onion sauce, stir in spinach, cracker or bread crumbs and cheese. Spoon into prepared mold; cover. Set dish in large pan and pour boiling water into pan halfway up dish. Bake in a preheated 350°F oven for 1 hour or until center is almost set. Remove from water. Serve warm or cold. To serve, place serving platter over dish, invert and turn out onto platter. Garnish with lemon slices, stuffed green olives or tomato roses.

Serves 8 to 10

MUSHROOM ROLL WITH LEMON SAUCE

"This is easy, different and adaptable. Serve with the lemon sauce, or fill with a crab meat and sour cream mixture. Good filled with creamed spinach, too . . ."

Vegetable oil
1½ pounds minced fresh
   mushrooms
6 eggs, separated
½ cup butter *or* margarine, melted
½ teaspoon salt

¼ teaspoon freshly ground white
   pepper
2 tablespoons fresh lemon juice
5 fresh mushrooms for garnish,
   sautéed
2 tablespoons chopped fresh parsley

Brush a jelly roll pan with vegetable oil; line with wax paper letting paper extend 3 inches on each end. Brush paper with vegetable oil and set pan aside. Put mushrooms in food processor and mince with metal blade or mince by hand.(If using food processor, mince about ¼ of the mushrooms at a time.) Put minced mushrooms in the corner of a dish towel, a handful at a time; wring out to remove excess moisture. Place mushrooms in a bowl. Beat egg yolks until fluffy. Add to mushrooms with melted butter or margarine, salt, pepper and lemon juice. (For a flavor change add 1 teaspoon dried tarragon or dried rosemary or 2 tablespoons fresh minced parsley to the mushroom mixture.) Beat egg whites until they form soft peaks; fold into mushroom mixture. Pour batter into prepared pan, spread evenly and bake in a preheated 350°F oven 20 to 25 minutes, or until mixture starts to pull away from sides of pan. Turn out onto 2 overlapping greased sheets of wax paper; using paper to help, roll up like a jelly roll. Prepare Lemon Sauce.

Lemon Sauce:
1 cup real mayonnaise
2 eggs
3 tablespoons fresh lemon juice

1 teaspoon grated lemon rind
½ teaspoon salt
1 teaspoon Dijon-style mustard

In small saucepan stir together all ingredients (with wire whisk) until smooth. Stir over medium-low heat until thick but do not let boil. Drizzle Lemon Sauce over roll and garnish with 5 sautéed mushrooms and chopped parsley.

Makes 1⅔ cups
Serves 8 to 10

APPLE STUFFED ACORN SQUASH — "Good autumny flavor in this dish; goes well with a roast."

APPLE STUFFED ACORN SQUASH

3 acorn squash	½ cup maple-flavored syrup
3 tart red apples	¼ cup butter *or* margarine, melted
1 cup broken cashew nuts	

Wash squash; cut in half lengthwise. Scoop out seeds and stringy substance. Wash, core and dice unpared apples. Combine with remaining ingredients. Fill squash halves with apple mixture. Brush surface with additional melted butter or margarine. Put in baking dish and pour in boiling water to depth of ½ inch. Cover dish with foil and bake in a preheated 400°F oven for 45 minutes. Uncover and bake an additional 10 minutes. Test squash with a fork to be sure it is tender.

Serves 6

?INACH AND CELERY MIX

...es in a tangy sauce."

...frozen

...y

...poons butter *or* margarine

1 tablespoon all-purpose flour
¼ teaspoon freshly ground pepper
½ cup half-and-half
2 tablespoons cream-style
    horseradish
¼ cup grated Parmesan cheese

Cook spinach according to package directions; drain well. Set aside. Combine celery, water and salt in saucepan; cover, cook rapidly 5 minutes. Remove cover and cook rapidly until liquid is absorbed. Add butter or margarine, blend in flour and pepper; add half-and-half and cook, stirring until sauce is thick and begins to bubble. Stir in horseradish and spinach; pour into greased 1½-quart casserole. Sprinkle with cheese. Bake in a preheated 375°F oven for 20 minutes or until heated through.

Serves 8

WALNUT BROCCOLI

"This is really good. It serves as a vegetable and bread for a dinner menu"

3 10½-ounce packages frozen
    chopped broccoli
½ cup butter *or* margarine
¼ cup all-purpose flour
2 teaspoons instant chicken
    bouillon

2 cups milk
⅔ cup water
6 tablespoons butter *or* margarine
⅔ of a 7-ounce package fine bread
    stuffing mix
⅔ cup chopped walnuts

Cook broccoli until just tender; drain and place in shallow greased 9x13-inch baking dish. Melt ½ cup butter or margarine; blend in flour and instant chicken bouillon; simmer, stirring, for 3 to 4 minutes. Blend in milk; cook, stirring until thickened. Pour over broccoli. Heat water and 6 tablespoons butter or margarine together and pour over stuffing; stir in nuts. Top broccoli with this mixture and bake in a preheated 400°F oven for 20 minutes or until thoroughly heated through and stuffing begins to brown.

Serves 8 to 10

SNOWY MASHED POTATOES

*"A tasty, different approach to mashed potatoes . . . can be |
before and refrigerated."*

8 to 10 russet potatoes, peeled and
quartered
1 8-ounce package cream cheese,
softened
1 cup dairy sour cream
½ cup minced scallions, including
some of the greens
½ cup minced celery

¼ cup minced greer
1 tablespoon mince(
¼ cup butter *or* margarine, melted
¼ teaspoon garlic powder
1 teaspoon salt *or* to taste
Freshly ground pepper to taste
½ teaspoon paprika
2 tablespoons butter *or* margarine

Cook potatoes in boiling salted water until tender. Drain and return pan to low
heat, shaking to dry potatoes. In large bowl of electric mixer, cream together
cheese and sour cream. Add hot potatoes one at a time to cream mixture and
continue beating at high speed until light and fluffy. On low speed add minced
scallions, celery, green pepper, parsley, ¼ cup melted butter or margarine, garlic
powder, salt and pepper. Spoon into a 2½ to 3-quart baking dish. Sprinkle with
paprika and dot with 2 tablespoons butter or margarine. Bake in a preheated
375°F oven for 25 minutes or until heated through and the top is golden.

Serves 8 to 10

ZUCCHINI FLAN

"Even if you normally don't like zucchini, you'll like this."

2 tablespoons butter *or* margarine
3 tablespoons chopped onion
1 tablespoon finely chopped scallions
6 small firm zucchini, stemmed,
sliced
1 cup heavy cream

3 eggs
¼ teaspoon ground nutmeg
Salt and freshly ground pepper to
taste
½ cup grated natural Swiss or
Cheddar cheese

Melt butter or margarine in saucepan, add onion and scallions and sauté 4 to
5 minutes. Add zucchini; sauté 5 minutes, turning over frequently. Spoon into
greased, shallow oven casserole; beat together cream, eggs, nutmeg, salt and
pepper to taste and pour over zucchini. Bake in a preheated 350°F oven for 20
minutes, covered. Uncover, sprinkle with cheese and bake 15 to 20 minutes
more or until set. Let cool 10 minutes before serving.

Serves 6 to 8

CANDIED SWEET POTATOES OR YAMS

A simplified and foolproof method of insuring that all the potatoes are candied and moist."

2 cups water	½ teaspoon ground nutmeg
2 cups sugar	1 slice lemon
¼ cup real butter	8 to 10 raw sweet potatoes *or* yams

Bring water and sugar to a boil; add butter, nutmeg and lemon slice, then add raw potatoes sliced ½ to ¾-inch thick; return to a boil. Reduce heat, cover and simmer until sweet potatoes are tender and cooked through, about 35 to 40 minutes.

Serves 10 to 12

CELERY SUPREME

"An interesting way to serve celery."

1 medium stalk celery, cut in 1-inch pieces (about 5 cups)	1 8-ounce can water chestnuts, drained and sliced
1 cup boiling salted water	1 4-ounce can pimiento, chopped
1 10¾-ounce can cream of mushroom soup, undiluted	1 cup grated Cheddar cheese

Add celery pieces to 1 cup boiling salted water; simmer for 10 minutes and drain. Combine drained celery with remaining ingredients except cheese. Turn into baking dish; sprinkle with grated cheese. Bake in a preheated 350°F oven for 25 to 30 minutes or until bubbly and cheese is melted.

Note: Be careful to cook celery until just barely tender — it should be slightly crisp in the finished dish.

Serves 6

GREEN BEAN CASSEROLE

"Try adding any of the leftovers from this casserole to an omelette

2 10½-ounce packages frozen
green beans
¼ cup butter or margarine
1 cup sliced celery
1 small onion, minced
1 tablespoon all-purpose flour
1 cup milk
½ cup half-and-half

Dash Tabasco® pepper sauce
2 teaspoons soy sauce
1 teaspoon salt
¼ teaspoon freshly ground pepper
4 ounces sharp Cheddar cheese,
grated
½ cup toasted chopped almonds

Prepare frozen green beans according to package directions. Melt butter or margarine in saucepan and add celery and onion; sauté until crisp-tender. Add flour; whisking slowly add milk and half-and-half. Continue cooking until thickened. Add Tabasco® pepper sauce, soy sauce, salt and pepper. Combine cooked green beans with sauce mixture in casserole. Sprinkle with grated cheese and chopped almonds. Bake in a preheated 375°F oven for 20 minutes or until hot and bubbly.

Serves 6

BRAISED CUCUMBER WITH DILLED SOUR CREAM

6 small cucumbers, peeled
Salt
6 tablespoons butter or margarine
1 small onion, minced
¼ cup dairy sour cream

2 tablespoons chopped fresh dill weed
or 2 teaspoons dried dill weed
Salt and freshly ground white pepper
to taste
¼ teaspoon ground nutmeg

Halve cucumbers lengthwise, sprinkle with salt and let stand for 20 minutes. Pat dry. Melt 4 tablespoons butter or margarine in saucepan, add cucumbers and simmer, covered, for 10 minutes or until tender, over low heat. Remove cucumbers to plate. Add remaining 2 tablespoons butter or margarine and onion to pan; simmer for 5 minutes. Remove from heat; stir in sour cream and dill weed. Check seasoning and add salt and pepper to taste; stir in nutmeg. Return cucumber to sauce in pan and bring to simmer. Serve hot.

Serves 4 to 6

BRAISED CUCUMBER WITH
DILLED SOUR CREAM — "A tasty
way to serve cooked cucumber."

MUSHROOM TART

"So tempting served with beef roast and tossed green salad. . ."

1 9-inch pie shell, baked 10 minutes
3 tablespoons butter *or* margarine
2 tablespoons chopped shallots
1 pound fresh mushrooms
¼ cup dry Madeira *or* dry sherry

2 tablespoons all-purpose flour
2 cups half-and-half
3 eggs, lightly beaten
2 tablespoons chopped fresh parsley

Prepare pie shell. Melt butter or margarine in large skillet. Add shallots and cook until soft. Wash mushrooms carefully; chop roughly in work bowl of food processor or by hand. If using processor, process in 3 batches to control size of mushroom pieces. Add mushrooms to skillet and cook until mixture looks dry. Add Madeira or sherry and cook until liquid evaporates. Sprinkle with flour and stir. Add half-and-half and heat until mixture thickens. Remove from heat and add 3 eggs, beaten lightly. Stir in chopped parsley. Pour into baked crust and bake 30 minutes in a preheated 350°F oven. Cool 10 minutes before cutting into serving wedges. Sprinkle with additional chopped parsley.

Serves 6

BROCCOLI WITH LEMON SAUCE

"A delicious sauce to heighten the flavor of broccoli . . ."

2 pounds fresh broccoli, cooked *or* 3 10½-ounce packages frozen
   broccoli spears, cooked

Lemon Sauce:
1 cup real mayonnaise
2 eggs
3 tablespoons fresh lemon juice

½ teaspoon salt
½ teaspoon dry mustard
¼ cup dairy sour cream
½ teaspoon paprika

In small saucepan, mix all sauce ingredients; stir with whisk and cook over medium-low heat until thick and smooth. Do not boil. Place hot, cooked broccoli on serving platter and drizzle sauce over the top. Dust with additional paprika.

Makes 1½ cups sauce
Serves 8 to 10

CARROTS AND MUSHROOMS

1 pound carrots
2 tablespoons butter *or* margarine
1 tablespoon olive oil
1 small onion, minced
1 clove garlic, minced
8 fresh mushrooms, sliced

Salt and freshly ground pepper to
 taste
¼ teaspoon dried rosemary, crushed
¼ teaspoon ground cardamom
2 to 4 tablespoons heavy cream

Scrape and slice carrots diagonally into thin slices. Combine butter or margarine, olive oil, onion and garlic in saucepan and sauté for 1 minute. Add carrots, mushrooms and seasonings and simmer, covered, over low heat for 15 minutes or until crisp-tender. Stir in cream and check seasoning.

Serves 6

CARROTS AND MUSHROOMS — "Serve with ham and a tossed green salad; a colorful and nutritional combination."

TURNIP FLUFF

"A nice change from the usual boiled and buttered turnips."

3 medium turnips, peeled and sliced
¾ teaspoon salt
⅛ teaspoon freshly ground pepper
⅛ teaspoon dried basil, crushed
Tabasco® pepper sauce to taste
1½ teaspoons grated lemon rind

2 tablespoons butter *or* margarine, melted
1 egg, separated
1 tablespoon firmly packed brown sugar

Cook turnips in boiling water until tender, about 15 minutes. Drain and mash. Season with salt, pepper, basil and Tabasco® pepper sauce. Add lemon rind and melted butter or margarine. Beat egg yolk and add. Let cool. Beat egg white until stiff; fold into turnips. Pour into well-greased 1-quart baking dish and sprinkle top with brown sugar. Bake uncovered in a preheated 350°F oven for 20 to 25 minutes.

Serves 4

CAULIFLOWER POLONAISE

"There's more than one way to fix cauliflower . . . and here is a good recipe . . ."

1 head cauliflower, trimmed
½ cup water
Salt to taste
½ cup butter *or* margarine
1 cup dry bread crumbs

Juice of ½ lemon
Salt and freshly ground pepper to taste
4 eggs, hard-cooked
½ cup fresh parsley, minced

Cook whole cauliflower in ½ cup boiling, salted water, covered for 20 minutes or until crisp-tender; drain and keep warm. In saucepan, melt butter or margarine, add bread crumbs and stir until golden; sprinkle with lemon juice, salt and pepper to taste. Keep warm. Mince hard-cooked eggs and mix with chopped parsley, salt and pepper to taste. Put cauliflower on heated platter and sprinkle with bread crumbs; surround with egg-parsley mixture.

Serves 6 to 8

SALADS

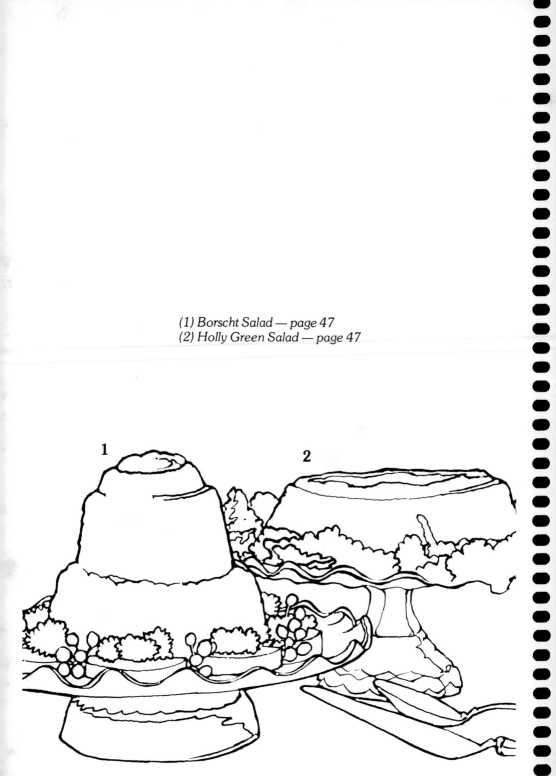

BORSCHT SALAD

"The color of a tree ornament . . . zingy taste, too."

1 1-pound 4-ounce can crushed
pineapple
1 6-ounce package raspberry-
flavored gelatin
1½ cups boiling water
1 1-pound can cubed beets

3 tablespoons cider vinegar
1 teaspoon dried dill weed
Dash salt
1 cup chopped celery
Dairy sour cream
Dill weed for garnish

Drain pineapple, reserving syrup. Dissolve gelatin in boiling water. Stir in beets with liquid, vinegar, dill, salt and reserved pineapple liquid. Chill until syrupy. Fold in celery and pineapple. Pour into 2-quart mold. Chill until firm. Top with sour cream and a sprinkle of dill weed.

Serves 8

HOLLY GREEN SALAD

"A fine blending of flavorings . . . a feast for the eyes and palate."

1 6-ounce package lime-flavored
gelatin
1¼ cups water
1 1-pound 4-ounce can crushed
pineapple
¼ teaspoon salt

1 teaspoon grated lime or lemon rind
½ teaspoon dried dill weed
½ cup dry vermouth
2 cups dairy sour cream
Green food coloring
Crisp salad greens

In saucepan, mix gelatin and water. Drain pineapple well, reserving juice. Add juice to gelatin with salt, lime or lemon rind and dill weed. Bring to boil stirring constantly to dissolve gelatin. Cool. Stir in vermouth and chill until gelatin is consistency of unbeaten egg white. Blend in sour cream, pineapple and a few drops of green food coloring to intensify color. Pour into 1½-quart ring mold. Chill until firm. Unmold onto crisp salad greens before serving.

Serves 6 to 8

TOMATO ASPIC

"The fresh taste of tomato comes through in this deep red aspic."

2 tablespoons unflavored gelatin
½ cup cool chicken broth (your own *or* canned)
4 cups tomato juice
½ cup chopped celery
¼ cup chopped scallions
2 tablespoons Worcestershire sauce
1 teaspoon celery seed
1 teaspoon salt
½ teaspoon sugar
Freshly ground white pepper to taste
3 tomatoes, peeled, seeded and cut into fine strips

In small bowl, sprinkle gelatin over chicken broth and soften for 10 minutes. In saucepan combine tomato juice, celery, scallions, Worcestershire sauce, celery seed, salt, sugar and white pepper. Simmer for 5 minutes. Add softened gelatin and stir until gelatin is dissolved. Set saucepan in cold water and stir to cool. Fold in tomatoes. Rinse a decorative 2-quart ring mold with cold water, pour in tomato mixture and chill, covered, for at least 4 hours or overnight. Unmold and serve on lettuce leaves with the following dressing.

Dill-Mayonnaise Dressing:
½ cup real mayonnaise
1 tablespoon fresh lemon juice
2 tablespoons dairy sour cream
½ teaspoon dried dill weed

Blend all ingredients well and let stand for an hour to develop flavors.

Serves 8 to 10

ASPARAGUS MIMOSA

3 10½-ounce packages frozen asparagus *or* 3½ pounds fresh asparagus

Sauce:
3 tablespoons chopped fresh parsley
3 tablespoons chopped chives
1 teaspoon dried tarragon
1 teaspoon dried basil
¼ cup wine vinegar
4 teaspoons Dijon-style mustard
¾ cup olive oil
Salt and freshly ground pepper to taste
2 eggs, hard-cooked and finely chopped

Cook asparagus until crisp-tender; drain. Put parsley, chives, tarragon, basil, vinegar, mustard and oil in blender. Blend until smooth. Pour over asparagus and let marinate 1 hour. Serve with eggs sprinkled over the top.

Serves 8

CINNAMON-APPLE SALAD

"Beautiful — and the perfect garnish for a yummy pork roast."

6 Winesap apples, cored, peeled, cut in half
4 cups water
½ cup sugar
1 stick cinnamon 3 inches long *or* ½ cup cinnamon red hot candies
6 to 8 drops red food coloring (if using cinnamon candies, omit food coloring)

2 3-ounce packages cream cheese, softened
½ cup chopped nuts
¼ cup dairy sour cream
1 tablespoon fresh lemon juice

Prepare apples. In large saucepan, mix water and sugar; add cinnamon stick and food coloring (or cinnamon red hot candies); bring to boil; simmer 10 minutes. Add apples and bring to simmer, basting frequently so apples will absorb color and flavor. Simmer for 10 to 15 minutes or until apples are cooked through but still retain their shape. Let cool in the syrup; remove and chill. Reserve syrup in which apples were cooked. Mix cream cheese, ¼ cup chopped nuts, sour cream and lemon juice until well blended. Roll into 12 balls. Roll each ball in reserved chopped nuts and place on each apple half. Reduce syrup in which apples were cooked until about ¾ cup remains. Cool and spoon 1 tablespoon over each apple half.

Serves 12

ASPARAGUS MIMOSA — "So good . . . looks pretty, too."

ARTICHOKES VINAIGRETTE — "A healthy, superb fresh salad!"

ARTICHOKES VINAIGRETTE

6 fresh artichokes
6 tablespoons olive oil
3 tablespoons cider *or* wine vinegar
1 clove garlic, minced
1 tablespoon salt

6 white peppercorns
1 bay leaf
¼ teaspoon dried thyme, crushed
Salt and freshly ground pepper to
    taste

Wash artichokes well, cut off stem of each at base. Trim off top ⅓ of each leaf with scissors; place in large enamel covered pot. Cover with water, add oil, vinegar and spices. Cook over high heat until base of artichokes can be easily pierced with a fork, or a bottom leaf can be easily removed — about 40 to 60 minutes depending on size of artichoke. Drain well, upside down, squeezing a bit to remove moisture. Spread leaves apart and remove choke with a spoon. Season with salt and pepper to taste. Prepare following vinaigrette sauce to serve in separate little saucers with the artichokes.

Vinaigrette:
½ cup olive *or* peanut oil
¼ cup cider *or* wine vinegar
½ teaspoon salt

Freshly ground pepper to taste
½ clove garlic, minced
1 teaspoon Dijon-style mustard
2 teaspoons capers

Put all ingredients except capers in blender and blend well. Add capers and refrigerate in covered jar until ready to serve.

Makes about ¾ cup sauce
Serves 6

WINTER FRUIT SALAD

"A delicious salad for dinner or for a ladies' luncheon served with finger sandwiches."

2 cups coarsely diced celery
3 cups coarsely diced, unpeeled Red Delicious apples
1 8-ounce can pineapple tidbits, canned in their own juice, well drained

2 11-ounce cans mandarin oranges, well drained
¾ cup salted, toasted almonds
1 banana, sliced (optional)

Toss the above ingredients in a bowl. Just before serving add one or the other of the following dressings and serve on crisp greens.

Serves 8

TART DRESSING

¾ cup real mayonnaise
¼ cup dairy sour cream
1 tablespoon fresh lemon juice

Mix above ingredients and add to the salad.

Makes 1 cup

CREAM AND MAYONNAISE DRESSING

1 cup real mayonnaise
½ cup heavy cream, whipped very stiff (being careful that it does not turn to butter)

Fold mayonnaise into whipped cream; add to the salad.

Makes 1½ cups

RED ONION AND SLICED ORANGE SALAD

4 large oranges
1 medium red onion
Salad greens

Dressing:

½ cup vegetable oil
¼ cup white vinegar
3 tablespoons sugar
½ teaspoon dry mustard
½ teaspoon paprika

1½ teaspoons Worcestershire
  sauce
½ teaspoon salt
⅛ teaspoon freshly ground pepper
½ teaspoon celery seed

Peel oranges through to fruit; horizontally slice evenly; allow 3 to 4 nice slices for each serving. Slice onion thinly and if strong, soak in cold water for a few minutes. Arrange salad greens on serving plates; place orange slices topped with onion rings. Blend all ingredients of dressing well. Spoon on dressing just before serving.

Serves 6 to 8

MOLDED CRANBERRY SALAD

"A tangy salad that brightens any holiday table."

2 cups cranberries, washed and
  picked over
1 small orange
1 6-ounce package lemon-flavored
  gelatin

1 cup sugar
¾ cup boiling water
1 cup orange juice
½ cup chopped nuts

Dressing:

½ cup real mayonnaise

1 teaspoon lemon rind
2 tablespoons orange juice

Coarsely grind cranberries. Quarter and seed unpeeled orange and grind; add to cranberries. Mix gelatin and sugar together; add to boiling water, stirring until dissolved. Stir in orange juice. Refrigerate until slightly jelled. Add cranberry-orange mixture and chopped nuts; mix well. Pour into decorative 6½-cup ring mold; let set for 4 hours or overnight. Unmold on lettuce leaves. Serve with a dressing of mayonnaise and lemon rind mixed and thinned with orange juice. Garnish with fresh or preserved kumquats, if desired.

Serves 8 to 10

RED ONION AND SLICED ORANGE SALAD — "Red onion really knows how to compliment oranges in color, texture and flavor in this easy creation."

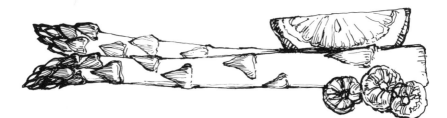

ASPARAGUS IN SHRIMP SAUCE

"A delicious, tempting and pretty salad . . ."

2 10½-ounce packages frozen asparagus *or* 2 pounds fresh asparagus
⅓ cup vegetable oil
⅓ cup fresh lemon juice
¼ teaspoon dried dill weed
¼ teaspoon dry mustard
½ teaspoon salt
¼ teaspoon freshly ground pepper
8 ounces tiny Alaskan shrimp, frozen *or* canned
Fresh parsley
Lemon slices

Cook asparagus until crisp-tender. Drain well. Arrange asparagus in shallow nonmetal dish. Mix oil, lemon juice, dill weed, dry mustard, salt and pepper in bowl. Add shrimp. Mix and pour over asparagus and let marinate for ½ to 1 hour, spooning some of the liquid over asparagus from time to time. Arrange on serving platter and garnish with parsley and lemon slices.

Serves 6 to 8

CAULIFLOWER AND BRUSSELS SPROUTS IN LEMON MAYONNAISE —
"These two members of the cabbage family come together delightfully
under this simple, tangy sauce."

CAULIFLOWER AND BRUSSELS SPROUTS IN LEMON-MAYONNAISE

1½ pounds cauliflower, separated in flowerettes

1 pound Brussels sprouts, cleaned, trimmed

Romaine lettuce leaves

Lemon slices

2 hard-cooked eggs, sieved

Place cauliflowerettes in saucepan in 1-inch boiling salted water; boil over high heat 2 minutes. Reduce to simmer; cook 5 minutes.* Drain. Place Brussels sprouts in saucepan in 1-inch boiling salted water; boil over high heat for 2 minutes. Reduce to simmer and cook 5 minutes.* Drain. Cool vegetables. When cold, combine with the following Lemon-Mayonnaise Sauce. Arrange on romaine leaves, garnish with thinly sliced lemon and sprinkle with the sieved eggs.

Lemon-Mayonnaise Sauce:

2 egg yolks

3 tablespoons fresh lemon juice

2 teaspoons Dijon-style mustard

½ teaspoon salt

Few drops Tabasco® pepper sauce

¾ cup olive oil

¾ cup vegetable oil

For Lemon-Mayonnaise Sauce: Place yolks, lemon juice, mustard, salt and Tabasco® pepper sauce in bowl of blender or processor; slowly add the oils until completely thickened. Check for seasoning. This should be a rather sharp mayonnaise.

*Note: These vegetables should be crisp-tender.

Serves 8

MARINATED VEGETABLE SALAD

"So simple to make with inexpensive ingredients."

1 1-pound can shoe peg corn
1 1-pound can sliced green beans
1 1-pound can very small peas
1 cup chopped celery
⅓ cup minced onion

½ cup white vinegar
⅓ cup vegetable oil
¾ cup sugar
Salt and freshly ground pepper to
taste

Drain all canned vegetables; add celery and onion and mix in a bowl. Heat vinegar, vegetable oil and sugar until sugar is dissolved; add salt and pepper to taste. Pour over vegetables and refrigerate for 24 hours before serving.

Serves 8 to 10

APPLE COLESLAW

"An effortless salad to have for a luncheon or dinner if made the night before."

4 cups finely shredded red or white
    cabbage *or* 2 cups each, mixed
1 Red Delicious apple, cored and
    finely shredded
1 4-ounce can pineapple tidbits,
    drained
½ cup heavy cream
½ cup dairy sour cream

3 tablespoons white wine vinegar
2 teaspoons sugar
¼ teaspoon salt
⅛ teaspoon freshly ground white
    pepper
1 Red Delicious apple, cored and
    thinly sliced, vertically
1½ tablespoons fresh lemon juice

In large bowl place shredded cabbage, shredded apple and pineapple tidbits. Toss to mix well. In small bowl, whip cream; fold in sour cream, vinegar, sugar, salt and white pepper. Toss with cabbage mixture and chill up to 8 hours before serving. Just before serving dip the pieces of thinly sliced apple in lemon juice and arrange as garnish over the salad.

Serves 8

RED AND GREEN ASPIC MOLD —
"So pretty for a holiday buffet."

RED AND GREEN ASPIC MOLD

Green (Avocado) Aspic:

1 envelope unflavored gelatin
¼ cup cold water
1 cup boiling water
1 teaspoon sugar
3 tablespoons fresh lemon juice
1 cup mashed avocado*

½ cup dairy sour cream
½ cup real mayonnaise
1 teaspoon salt
⅛ teaspoon freshly ground white pepper
⅛ teaspoon cayenne pepper

Soften gelatin in cold water; pour into boiling water and stir until dissolved. Add sugar and 1 tablespoon of lemon juice. Chill until slightly thickened. Mash avocado (if fresh); add remaining 2 tablespoons lemon juice, sour cream, mayonnaise, salt, pepper and cayenne. Mix thoroughly with slightly thickened gelatin. Pour into a 1½ or 2-quart mold. Chill until set.

*Note: Frozen avocado dip may be used if you can't find ripe, fresh avocados. Add a drop or two of green food coloring to avocado mix if desired.

Tomato Aspic:

1 envelope unflavored gelatin
¼ cup cold water
1 cup boiling water

2 tablespoons sugar
1 10-ounce can tomato soup
1 tablespoon fresh lemon juice
¼ teaspoon salt

Soften gelatin in cold water; dissolve in boiling water. Add sugar, soup, lemon juice and salt. Cool to room temperature. Pour over firm avocado aspic. Chill for 4 hours or until set. Unmold on salad greens.

Note: Double the recipe if using an 8-cup tree mold.

Serves 8 to 10

MOLDED AVOCADO-GRAPEFRUIT SALAD

"Try adding paper-thin slices of pimiento or red apple for a color highlight."

1 6-ounce package lime-flavored gelatin
3½ cups boiling water
¼ cup fresh lemon juice
2 tablespoons cream-style horseradish

2 teaspoons grated onion
2 ripe avocados, sliced
2 grapefruits, sectioned
Real mayonnaise
Half-and-half

Pour boiling water over gelatin in large bowl. Stir until dissolved. Add lemon juice, horseradish and grated onion. Refrigerate until gelatin begins to set. With electric beater, beat until light and fluffy. Put a thin layer of gelatin in a 6½-cup mold. Layer in fruits and cover with remaining gelatin. Refrigerate until completely set. Unmold and garnish with salad greens. Serve drizzled with mayonnaise thinned with half-and-half.

Serves 12

BREADS

RAISIN BREAD

"Delicious and healthful — a special treat toasted for a holiday breakfast."

2 cups all-purpose flour
2 packages active dry yeast
½ cup sugar
1 teaspoon salt
½ teaspoon ground cinnamon
½ teaspoon ground allspice
½ teaspoon ground nutmeg
2 cups milk

¾ cup water
¼ cup vegetable oil
4 cups whole wheat flour
1 cup rolled oats
1 cup raisins
1 to 1½ cups all-purpose flour
1 tablespoon real butter, melted

In large mixing bowl, combine first 7 ingredients and blend on low speed of electric mixer or by hand. Heat milk, water and oil until very warm (120° to 130°F). Combine the warm liquid with flour mixture on low speed until moistened; beat 4 minutes at medium speed, or do the equivalent by hand. With dough hook of mixer, or by hand, stir in whole wheat flour, oats, raisins and enough white flour to make a stiff dough. On well-floured surface, knead dough until smooth and elastic, about 5 to 7 minutes.

Place in greased bowl; turn over to grease underside. Cover, let rise in warm place 30 minutes only. Grease 2 8½x4½x2½-inch loaf pans. Punch dough down; divide and shape into 2 loaves. Place in greased pans; brush with melted butter. Cover; let rise in warm place until doubled in size, about 45 minutes. Bake in preheated 350°F oven for 40 to 50 minutes or until loaf sounds hollow when lightly tapped. Remove from pans. If desired brush with butter and sprinkle with sugar.

Makes 2 loaves

CRANBERRY-ORANGE-NUT BREAD

"The traditional autumn flavors of cranberry and orange combine to make this delicious nut bread . . ."

4 cups all-purpose flour
1½ cups sugar
1 tablespoon baking powder
1 teaspoon salt
1 teaspoon baking soda
2 cups cranberries, washed, picked
over, cut in halves

1 cup walnuts or pecans,
chopped
2 teaspoons grated orange rind
2 eggs, beaten
1½ cups orange juice
½ cup vegetable oil

Sift together dry ingredients. Stir in cranberries, nuts and orange rind. Combine eggs, orange juice and vegetable oil. Add to dry ingredients, stirring until just moistened. Divide batter into 3 lightly greased and floured 7½x3½x3¼-inch loaf pans. Bake in a preheated 375°F oven for 45 to 50 minutes or until done.

Makes 3 loaves

SWEDISH COFFEE RING

1 package active dry yeast
¼ cup lukewarm water (105° to 115°F)
⅓ cup + ½ teaspoon sugar
⅓ cup butter *or* margarine
½ teaspoon salt
½ cup milk, scalded
1 egg, beaten
½ cup cold mashed potatoes
3 cups all-purpose flour
2 tablespoons butter *or* margarine, melted

Soften yeast in warm water; stir in ½ teaspoon sugar. In large mixing bowl, combine ⅓ cup sugar, butter or margarine, salt and scalded milk; cool to lukewarm. Blend in egg, mashed potatoes and yeast. Gradually add flour to form a stiff dough, beating well after each addition. Knead on floured surface 3 to 5 minutes. Place in greased bowl, turning dough to grease all sides. Cover; let rise in warm place (85° to 90°F) until doubled, about 1 hour. Punch dough down. Cover. Store in refrigerator at least 2 hours (not over 3 days). When ready to bake, punch dough down, divide in 2 portions and mold into balls; roll out each portion into an 18x10-inch rectangle. Brush each with 1 tablespoon melted butter or margarine. Prepare following filling.

Filling:
1 cup chopped nuts
1 cup sugar
1 teaspoon ground cardamom
1 teaspoon ground cinnamon
½ cup currants or raisins soaked in
¼ cup rum *or* fruit-flavored liqueur (optional)

Sprinkle each rectangle with filling. Place a sheet of wax paper over the sprinkled dough; roll with rolling pin over the paper to push the filling into the dough. Remove wax paper. Roll as for a jelly roll, starting with 18-inch side. Place each roll on a greased baking sheet; shape into a ring, overlapping the ends. Snip sections with kitchen scissors 1½ inches apart, cutting each to within 1 inch of center. Turn each cut section slightly to one side to form a wreath. Let rise in warm place until doubled, about 45 minutes. Bake in a preheated 350°F oven for 25 to 30 minutes, until golden brown. When cool prepare Almond Glaze, below:

Almond Glaze:
2 cups confectioners' sugar
2 tablespoons butter *or* margarine, softened
¼ cup milk
½ teaspoon almond extract

Combine all ingredients and blend until smooth. Dribble over coffee ring.

Note: This can also be made in 2 greased 6½-cup ring molds and the top snipped with scissors.

Makes 2 rings

COCONUT-PUMPKIN LOAF

"A moist, tasty bread . . ."

2 cups sugar
2 cups all-purpose flour
1 teaspoon baking soda
1 teaspoon salt
1 teaspoon ground cinnamon
1 teaspoon ground nutmeg
⅔ cup flaked coconut

2 3½-ounce packages coconut
  pie filling (regular)
5 eggs
1½ cups vegetable oil
2 cups cooked pumpkin (about 1
  pound)

Mix together the first 8 ingredients in a large mixing bowl. In another bowl, mix together eggs, vegetable oil and cooked pumpkin, blending well. Add egg mixture to dry ingredients; mix well. Grease 2 8½x4½x2½-inch loaf pans and cover bottoms with greased wax paper. Divide batter evenly between pans and place on middle rack of a preheated 350°F oven. Bake for 50 minutes to 1 hour and 10 minutes. Tester should come out clean. Cool in pan for 10 minutes. Carefully turn out onto cake rack and remove wax paper; cool completely.

Note: This bread freezes well.

Makes 2 loaves

SWEDISH COFFEE RING — "A warm piece of coffee ring and a steaming cup of hot coffee — a lovely way to welcome guests."

DATE-NUT BREAD

"Try adding your own choice of fruit to this easy and quick holiday yeast bread."

4 to 5 cups all-purpose flour	¼ cup vegetable oil
½ cup sugar	1 egg
2 teaspoons salt	2 tablespoons grated lemon *or*
2 packages active dry yeast	orange rind
1 cup orange juice	1 cup chopped dates
1 cup milk	½ cup coarsely chopped pecans

In large mixer bowl, combine 2 cups flour, sugar, salt and yeast. In saucepan, heat orange juice, milk and vegetable oil to 120° to 130°F. Add warm liquid mixture and egg to flour mixture and blend at low speed until moistened; beat for 4 minutes at medium speed. Blend in lemon or orange rind. Blend in 2 to 3 cups flour with pastry hook or blend in by hand. Dough will be stiff. Cover and let rise in warm place until light and doubled in size, about 40 to 60 minutes. Meanwhile, grease a 10-inch tube pan using solid shortening or margarine. Arrange chopped dates and nuts on bottom of greased pan. Punch dough down and place in prepared pan. Bake 50 to 60 minutes in a preheated 350°F oven or until golden brown and loaf sounds hollow when tapped. Remove from pan. Cool for 20 minutes; prepare following glaze.

Glaze:	1 tablespoon fresh lemon juice
1 cup confectioners' sugar	1 tablespoon water (approximately)

Mix sugar, lemon juice and water until proper consistency; spoon over fruit side of loaf.

Note: This batter rises only once and can be mixed partially or totally in an electric mixer. If this bread is not eaten straight out of the oven, reheat wrapped in foil.

CHRISTMAS STOLLEN

"Because this is a heavy dough, it takes a little longer to rise than might be expected . . . but well worth the wait."

1 cup milk	1 tablespoon fresh lemon juice
½ cup sugar	2 teaspoons grated lemon rind
¾ teaspoon salt	½ teaspoon grated cardamom
½ cup real butter	½ teaspoon each, ground cinnamon,
2 packages active dry yeast	nutmeg and cloves
¼ cup lukewarm water	2 eggs + 1 egg yolk
1 tablespoon sugar	¼ cup each, candied citron, orange
1 cup unbleached flour	peel, lemon peel and cherries
1 cup currants *or* ½ cup each,	5 to 6 cups unbleached flour
currants and raisins	1 tablespoon real butter, melted
1 tablespoon rum *or* brandy	Candied fruit for decorating

In small saucepan, mix together milk, ½ cup sugar, salt and butter; bring to boil, stirring. Remove from heat; cool to lukewarm.

In large bowl of electric mixer combine dry yeast, lukewarm water and 1 tablespoon sugar mixing to dissolve; let stand 5 minutes. Stir in 1 cup unbleached flour and cooled milk-sugar mixture. Let stand in warm place until bubbly, about ½ hour.

Meanwhile, mix currants (or currants and raisins) with rum or brandy, lemon juice and rind; add the 4 spices. Let stand, stirring from time to time.

When yeast mixture is bubbly, stir in eggs and yolk, currants (or currants and raisins), candied fruits and 5 of the 6 cups of flour. If using a dough hook on electric mixer, beat at low speed for 5 to 6 minutes or blend by hand. Dough will be sticky and rather soft; turn dough out onto well floured board. Knead in the last cup of flour by hand and continue kneading for 4 to 5 minutes. Place dough in well oiled bowl and turn dough over to cover with oil. Cover with a dampened dish towel and let rise in a warm place until double in bulk, about 1½ hours.

Punch dough down, knead for 1 minute, divide in half and shape into long oval loaves. Brush top with melted butter and place on well oiled baking sheet. Cover with a dampened dish towel, let rise in warm place until double in bulk, about 1 hour.

Bake in a preheated 375°F oven for 50 minutes or until lightly brown and hollow sounding when tapped. When cold, prepare following glaze.

Glaze:
1 cup sifted confectioners' sugar

¼ teaspoon vanilla
1½ tablespoons milk

Mix together adding a bit more milk if necessary to make good consistency for spreading. Coat loaves with glaze and decorate with a few pieces of candied fruit before glaze sets.

Note: This sounds like a complicated recipe but it isn't. It's fun to knead bread, but the work is shortened with a dough hook attachment of an electric mixer. These loaves make lovely Christmas presents, too!

Makes 2 loaves

BUBBLE BREAD

1 cup milk, scalded	2 packages active dry yeast
½ cup vegetable shortening	2 eggs, beaten
1 teaspoon salt	4½ cups all-purpose flour
½ cup sugar	

Mix milk, shortening, salt and sugar together in medium-size bowl and stir until sugar is dissolved. When milk mixture is 98° to 105°F, add yeast and stir until dissolved. Add beaten eggs and flour; mix to make a soft dough. Turn out onto floured board and knead until smooth. Place in a greased bowl, cover and let rise until double in size. Punch dough down and let rise 10 minutes.

Sugar-Fruit Topping:

2 tablespoons butter *or* margarine	2 tablespoons light corn syrup
½ cup firmly packed brown sugar	½ cup candied cherry halves

For Sugar-Fruit Topping: Combine 2 tablespoons butter or margarine, brown sugar and light corn syrup. Spread in greased Bundt or tube pan and place candied cherries with cut side up in pan.

Coating:

½ cup butter *or* margarine, melted	1½ teaspoons ground cinnamon
1½ cups sugar	½ cup finely chopped nuts
	½ cup raisins (optional)

For coating: Put ½ cup melted butter or margarine in a shallow dish; in another bowl mix sugar, cinnamon, nuts and optional raisins. Make dough into balls the size of walnuts. Dip each in butter or margarine and then roll in cinnamon-nut mixture. Place in pan. Stagger in rows and layers. Let rise 45 minutes or until double in bulk and bake in a preheated 350°F oven for 45 minutes or until done. Turn out of pan immediately.

BUBBLE BREAD — "Makes a nice bread served with coffee when guests drop in!"

FAVORITE HOLIDAY BREAD

"These are great wrapped in holiday paper and given as gifts."

2 cups all-purpose flour
2 teaspoons baking soda
2 teaspoons ground cinnamon
1½ cups sugar
2 teaspoons salt

2 7½-ounce jars junior-sized
carrots (baby food)
½ cup vegetable oil
4 eggs, well beaten
½ cup chopped pecans *or* walnuts

Mix dry ingredients; add carrots, oil, beaten eggs and nuts. Mix and bake in 2 greased and floured 7½x3½x3¼-inch loaf pans in a preheated 375°F oven for 45 to 50 minutes or until done.

Note: This batter is rather thin.

Makes 2 loaves

PRUNE BREAD

"Try this bread smothered in whipped cream cheese and made into finger sandwiches — can't be beat."

½ cup butter *or* margarine
1½ cups sugar
2 eggs
2½ cups all-purpose flour
1 teaspoon baking powder
1 teaspoon baking soda

1 teaspoon ground cloves
1 teaspoon ground allspice
1 teaspoon ground cinnamon
1 cup buttermilk
1 cup chopped, cooked prunes
½ to 1 cup chopped black walnuts

In large mixing bowl cream butter or margarine and sugar together until light and fluffy. Beat in eggs one at a time. In a separate bowl, sift flour, baking powder, baking soda and spices together. Alternately add dry ingredients and buttermilk to creamed mixture. Fold in cooked prunes and nuts. Grease 2 7½x3½x3¼-inch loaf pans; cut and place a piece of greased wax paper to line the bottom of each. Dust with flour and divide batter between pans. Bake in a preheated 350°F oven for 50 minutes to 1 hour or until done. Let cool in pan for 10 minutes. Turn out onto cake rack and remove wax paper; cool completely.

Makes 2 loaves

KUGELHOPF

"A creation of nuts and fruit! Serve with a glass of Hot Cranberry Punch (page 98) if you like . . ."

½ cup dark raisins
½ cup currants
1 cup blanched almonds, finely chopped
1 tablespoon grated fresh lemon rind
1 tablespoon brandy
1 cup milk
1 cup sugar

1 package active dry yeast
½ cup warm water (105° to 115°F)
5 cups all-purpose flour
10 to 12 whole blanched almonds
1 cup butter *or* margarine, softened
1 teaspoon salt
6 eggs
¼ cup butter *or* margarine, melted
Confectioners' sugar

In small bowl, combine raisins, currants, ¾ cup chopped almonds, lemon rind and brandy; toss lightly, set aside. In small saucepan, heat milk to scalding; remove from heat. Stir in ¼ cup sugar; stir until dissolved; cool to lukewarm. Sprinkle yeast over warm water in large bowl; stir until dissolved. Stir in milk mixture and 3 cups flour; beat about 2 minutes until smooth. Cover bowl and let rise in warm place until light and spongy and double in bulk. Generously grease a Bundt pan. Sprinkle inside with reserved ¼ cup finely chopped almonds, turning pan round and round to distribute evenly. Place a whole almond in each indentation in bottom of Bundt pan. Set aside.

In large bowl, with electric mixer at medium speed, beat softened butter with remaining ¾ cup sugar and salt until light and fluffy. Beat in eggs, one at a time, until smooth. At low speed, beat in 1 cup remaining flour and the risen batter until smooth and well-blended. With wooden spoon stir in remaining flour and fruit-nut mixture. Mix until well combined. Pour into prepared mold. Cover; let rise in warm place until batter rises to top of pan, about 1 hour. Bake for 50 to 60 minutes in a preheated 350°F oven or until cake tester inserted near middle comes out clean. Let cool in pan on wire rack 20 minutes; loosen edges and turn out onto wire rack. Brush with melted butter or margarine. To store, when completely cold, wrap in wax paper, then in foil.

Serve at room temperature sprinkled lightly with confectioners' sugar.

Note: Will keep in refrigerator up to 2 weeks and in freezer indefinitely. If this bread is not eaten straight out of the oven, reheat wrapped in foil.

*DANISH AEBELSKIVER —
"Add a delightful twist
to breakfast with these
simple Aebelskivers."*

DANISH AEBELSKIVER

3 eggs
1 tablespoon sugar
½ teaspoon ground cardamom
4 cups all-purpose flour
3½ cups buttermilk

1 tablespoon baking soda
Butter or margarine for frying
Preserves, maple syrup or
  applesauce
Confectioners' sugar

Beat eggs, sugar and cardamom. Add flour and 3 cups buttermilk and blend until smooth. Dissolve baking soda in remaining ½ cup buttermilk; stir into batter. Put about ½ teaspoon butter or margarine in each cavity of the Aebelskiver iron. When bubbly hot, drop in about a level tablespoon of dough. When browned and puffed, turn over with a skewer and brown other side. Serve these little browned puffs of dough with either preserves, maple syrup or applesauce and a dusting of confectioners' sugar. If you like, add a little grated sharp cheese to the dough for a different taste treat.

Note: An Aebelskiver iron is of Danish origin, made of heavy metal, in which a small amount of batter is placed in each of several round indentations. The resultant little muffins are garnished in several ways and served for breakfast or dessert. These are obtainable in most kitchen or Scandinavian shops.

Makes about 6 dozen

MAYONNAISE MUFFINS

| 2 cups self-rising flour | 1 cup milk |
| ¼ cup real mayonnaise | 1 tablespoon sugar |

Combine ingredients and spoon into a greased muffin pan. Bake in a preheated 400°F oven for 15 to 20 minutes. Should be golden in color.

Suggestion: Put a layer of batter in muffin pan; add a teaspoon of marmalade or any kind of jelly or jam, then top with another layer of batter. May be reheated wrapped in foil.

Makes 12 muffins

FRENCH BREAKFAST PUFFS (right) — "A new twist to breakfast your family and guests will welcome." MAYONNAISE MUFFINS — "Very good — so light and tender."

FRENCH BREAKFAST PUFFS

½ cup sugar
⅓ cup butter or margarine
1 egg
1½ cups all-purpose flour
1½ teaspoons baking powder
½ teaspoon salt

¼ teaspoon ground nutmeg
½ cup milk
6 tablespoons butter or margarine
½ cup sugar
1 teaspoon ground cinnamon

In large mixing bowl, cream together ½ cup sugar, ⅓ cup butter or margarine and egg. In a separate bowl, sift together flour, baking powder, salt and nutmeg. Add to creamed mixture alternately with milk, beating well after each addition. Spoon into a greased muffin pan about ⅔ full. Bake in a preheated 350°F oven for 20 to 25 minutes. In small saucepan, melt butter or margarine. Combine ½ cup sugar and cinnamon in saucer. Remove muffins from oven; immediately dip tops in melted butter or margarine, then in cinnamon-sugar mixture to coat the tops. Serve warm.

Note: Muffins may be reheated wrapped in foil.

Makes 12 muffins

GOLDEN MUFFINS

"So good — may be made ahead and reheated wrapped in foil . . ."

1 8¼-ounce can crushed pineapple
2 cups sifted all-purpose flour
¼ cup sugar
1 tablespoon baking powder
¼ teaspoon salt

¼ teaspoon ground nutmeg
1 egg
1 cup milk
1 teaspoon grated orange rind
¼ cup real butter, melted

Drain pineapple very well, pressing against sides of sieve to remove moisture. Sift together flour, sugar, baking powder, salt and nutmeg. Beat together egg and milk; stir in pineapple and orange rind. Blend into dry ingredients by hand, along with melted butter, mixing as little as possible until all particles are moistened. Spoon into lightly greased muffin pan. Bake in a preheated 400°F oven 20 to 25 minutes, until golden. Remove to wire rack to cool 5 minutes before removing from pan. Serve warm.

Makes 12 muffins

REFRIGERATOR BISCUITS

"Refrigerator breads traditionally have an extra light texture . . . an added bonus to the fact that they're so easy."

2 cups buttermilk
1 package active dry yeast
1 teaspoon baking soda
1 teaspoon salt
1 teaspoon baking powder

1 teaspoon cream of tartar
2 tablespoons sugar
4 cups all-purpose flour
1 cup butter *or* margarine

Heat buttermilk to lukewarm and add yeast; stir until dissolved. Cool. Mix and sift dry ingredients into bowl. Cut in butter or margarine until size of small peas. When buttermilk is cool, mix with dry ingredients. Put in covered container and refrigerate until ready to use. Roll dough and cut into biscuits. Let rise 20 to 30 minutes before baking in a preheated 450°F oven for 10 minutes.

Note: A most unusual recipe. Dough keeps covered in the refrigerator for at least 5 days.

Makes about 24 small biscuits

HERB CASSEROLE BREAD

"So flavorful when pieces are lightly toasted and spread with butter . . ."

2 packages active dry yeast
2 cups warm water (105° to 115°F)
2 tablespoons sugar
1 teaspoon salt

2 tablespoons soft butter *or* margarine
1 .7-ounce package dry salad
   dressing mix (onion, Italian *or* other)
4½ cups all-purpose flour

Sprinkle yeast over water in large bowl of electric mixer; let stand a few minutes; stir to dissolve. Add sugar, salt, butter or margarine, salad dressing mix and 3 cups flour. Beat at low speed until blended. Beat at high speed until smooth, about 2 minutes. Scrape down side of bowl with spatula as necessary. With wooden spoon, gradually beat in rest of flour until blended. Dough will be sticky. Cover bowl with greased wax paper, then with towel. Let rise in warm place about 1 hour or until light and bubbly and more than double in volume. With wooden spoon, stir down batter; beat vigorously ½ minute or 30 strokes. Turn into a well greased, round 2-quart soufflé dish. Let dough rise for 30 to 40 minutes. Bake at 375°F for 50 minutes or until nicely browned and hollow sounding when tapped with knuckle. Turn out onto wire rack; cool completely or serve slightly warm cut into wedges.

Makes 1 loaf

DESSERTS

(1) Steamed Plum Pudding with Lemon Sauce — page 87
(2) Chocolate Torte — page 79
(3) Cranberry Upside Down Cake with Creme Chantilly — page 82

BAKED PLUM PUDDING WITH SAUCE

"An easy version of the traditional steamed pudding, but just as tasty."

1½ cups golden raisins	6 eggs
1½ cups currants	3 cups cornflake crumbs
1½ cups pecans	2 teaspoons ground cinnamon
¼ cup dark rum *or* brandy	½ teaspoon ground cloves
½ cup butter *or* margarine	½ teaspoon ground mace
1 cup sugar	½ teaspoon ground allspice

Two hours or longer before baking (even the night before), place raisins, currants, pecans and rum or brandy in jar with cover. Shake from time to time so fruit and nuts will be in contact with rum or brandy.

Beat butter or margarine in large bowl of electric mixer until creamy; gradually add sugar; add eggs one at a time, beating well after each addition. Combine cornflake crumbs with spices; stir in fruit and nut mixture. Carefully mix this into the creamed butter or margarine mixture being sure that fruits are well distributed. Spoon into a 10-inch angel food tin or a Bundt pan which has been well greased and dusted with flour. Place a round of greased wax paper over top of batter. Bake in a preheated 375°F oven for 30 to 40 minutes. Cool for 10 minutes in pan. Turn out onto cake rack and remove wax paper. Serve either warm or at room temperature with one of the following sauces.

Serves 10

SPICY BUTTER SAUCE

⅔ cup sugar	¼ cup real butter
1½ tablespoons cornstarch	½ teaspoon ground nutmeg
1 cup water	1 teaspoon vanilla

Combine sugar and cornstarch in a small saucepan; stir in water. Cook over medium heat, stirring constantly until thick and clear. Add butter, nutmeg and vanilla; blend well. Serve hot.

Note: Rum or brandy, added to taste, may be used as flavoring instead of vanilla.

HARD SAUCE

½ cup real butter	1 teaspoon vanilla
¯2 cups sifted confectioners' sugar	1 egg, separated

Thoroughly cream butter and confectioners' sugar together. Add vanilla and well beaten egg yolk. Beat egg white until stiff; fold into the creamed mixture. Chill.

ORANGE CAKE

"This is the grand lady of orange cakes . . ."

Juice and grated rind of 1 orange
½ cup sugar
½ cup real butter
2 eggs

1 cup less 2 tablespoons all-purpose
   flour
1 teaspoon baking powder
½ cup confectioners' sugar

In bowl of mixer, cream sugar and butter together until light and fluffy; add grated rind. Add eggs one at a time, beating well after each addition. Sift flour and baking powder together; fold into creamed mixture just until well blended. Do not beat or cake will be tough. Butter and flour an 8-inch cake pan. Pour in batter, pushing batter out from middle, leaving a slight indentation in center. (This makes cake bake evenly without peak in center.) Bake in a preheated 350°F oven for 25 minutes. Allow to cool for 10 minutes; turn out onto cake rack.

For glaze: Mix reserved orange juice and confectioners' sugar together. Spoon this mixture over warm cake, a little at a time. Repeat until all glaze is used up. If filling is desired, cake can be split in two when cold and filled with the following:

Orange Filling:
6 tablespoons butter *or* margarine
1⅔ cups sugar
2 eggs + 2 egg yolks

Grated rind of 1 orange
¼ cup orange juice
1 tablespoon Grand Marnier

In small saucepan, mix all ingredients except Grand Marnier. Constantly whisk over low heat until mixture thickens and coats a metal spoon, about 5 minutes. Take care: don't let mixture boil or cook without stirring or the eggs might scramble. Remove from heat, whisking to cool. Stir in Grand Marnier. Split cake in half horizontally and fill with this orange filling. Spoon glaze over top.

Note: This cake does not need any adjustments for high altitude.

Serves 6 to 8

CRANBERRY PUDDING

"The tasty contrast between tart cranberries and sweetened cream gives your tastebuds a delightful surprise."

1 cup all-purpose flour	2 tablespoons butter or margarine,
1 teaspoon baking powder	melted
½ cup sugar	1½ cups whole raw cranberries,
½ cup milk	picked over and washed

Mix together flour, baking powder and sugar; add milk, melted butter or margarine and cranberries. Pour into greased 8-inch round or square baking dish and bake in a 350°F preheated oven for 30 minutes or until tester comes out clean. Prepare following sauce:

Sauce: Ground nutmeg
Sugar   1 cup half-and-half

Add sugar and nutmeg to half-and-half to taste. Serve pudding warm topped with sauce.

Serves 6 to 8

COFFEE TORTE

"This one always gets rave reviews."

6 egg whites at room temperature	1 teaspoon almond extract
¼ teaspoon cream of tartar	¼ teaspoon ground allspice
1 cup sugar	¼ teaspoon ground mace
1½ cups sifted confectioners' sugar	

Beat egg whites until foamy; add cream of tartar, beat until whites hold a stiff peak. Continue beating and slowly add sugars, beating well between each addition. Add extract, allspice and mace and beat 2 minutes longer. Cut 4 8-inch circles from heavy paper. Divide meringue into 4 equal parts and spread evenly with spatula on circles. Place on baking sheets; bake in a preheated 250°F oven for 1 hour 15 minutes. Remove from oven; cool, then carefully remove paper from meringues.

Filling:	1 tablespoon all-purpose flour
6 egg yolks	½ cup real butter, softened
½ cup sugar	2 cups heavy cream, whipped
½ cup cold strong coffee	2 teaspoons cocoa

For filling: Combine egg yolks, sugar, coffee and flour in double boiler. Cook over boiling water, stirring constantly until mixture thickens. Cool to lukewarm. Add butter by spoonfuls and beat until smooth and satiny. Spread filling over top of 3 meringue layers; stack layers ending with unfilled layer. Spread whipped cream over top and sides. Sieve cocoa over the top in a light dusting. Chill 4 hours or overnight before serving.

Serves 8 to 12

GRASSHOPPER DESSERT SOUFFLÉ

1 package unflavored gelatin
½ cup water
½ cup sugar
⅛ teaspoon salt
3 egg yolks
¼ cup green creme de menthe

¼ cup white creme de cacao
1 cup heavy cream
3 egg whites at room temperature
Grated chocolate, chopped pistachio
    nuts *or* maraschino cherries

Fold a sheet of aluminum foil into a strip about 6 inches wide and long enough to go around a 1-quart soufflé dish. Press foil around dish, extending it above top of dish to make a "collar" about 2 inches high. Secure foil with tape.

Sprinkle gelatin over water. Let stand until gelatin is softened. Add ¼ cup sugar, salt and egg yolks. Mix well. Cook over moderate heat, stirring constantly, about 5 minutes or until mixture thickens slightly. Remove from heat. Add creme de menthe and creme de cacao. Mix well. Refrigerate, stirring occasionally, until it is barely thickened. Whip cream until stiff peaks form. Beat egg whites until foamy then gradually add remaining ¼ cup sugar. Continue to beat until stiff peaks form. Fold into gelatin mixture. Fold in whipped cream, lightly but thoroughly. Spoon mixture into soufflé dish. Refrigerate until firm. Remove foil collar to serve. Decorate with grated chocolate, chopped pistachio nuts or maraschino cherries.

Serves 8

CHOCOLATE TORTE

"So easy to make yet a real treat for chocolate lovers."

¾ cup butter *or* margarine
1½ cups sugar
3 eggs, separated
¾ cup milk

Pinch salt
1½ ounces unsweetened chocolate
1½ teaspoons vanilla
1½ cups all-purpose flour

Cream butter or margarine and sugar together until light and fluffy. Beat in egg yolks. Put milk and salt in small saucepan, add chocolate cut in bits and heat until melted, stirring. Cool. Add vanilla. Fold in flour alternately with milk mixture, ending with flour. Beat egg whites until stiff, but not dry. Fold into batter. Grease 3 8-inch round pans and smooth batter into pans. Bake in a preheated 350°F oven for 25 to 30 minutes. Cool for 10 minutes before turning out onto cake rack to cool completely. When cold frost with the following:

Frosting:
2 tablespoons butter *or* margarine
2 ounces unsweetened chocolate

2 tablespoons heavy cream
2 cups confectioners' sugar

For frosting: Melt together butter or margarine, chocolate and cream; mix in confectioners' sugar with enough additional cream to make spreading consistency. Frost bottom layers; spread remainder on top and sprinkle with sieved powdered sugar.

Serves 10 to 12

GINGER-PUMPKIN DESSERT

"A different way to serve a fall favorite . . ."

1 cup cooked pumpkin
½ cup sugar
¼ teaspoon salt
½ teaspoon ground ginger
½ teaspoon ground cinnamon

¼ teaspoon ground nutmeg
½ cup chopped pecans
1 quart best vanilla ice cream,
   softened
16 ginger snaps, crushed

Combine pumpkin, sugar, salt, spices and nuts. Stir into softened ice cream. Grease a 10x6x1½-inch dish. Line bottom with piece of wax paper cut to fit. Grease wax paper. Sprinkle with ½ of crushed ginger snaps and smooth ice cream mixture on top. Top with remaining ginger snaps. Freeze. Before serving, loosen sides with spatula and turn out onto plate. Peel off wax paper and cut into serving pieces.

Serves 6 to 8

GRASSHOPPER DESSERT SOUFFLÉ — "Make sure your guests see this lovely green soufflé before serving."

ORANGE BLOSSOM BOWL

"A light, smooth-flavored finish to any meal."

2 tablespoons honey
6 tablespoons frozen orange juice,
   thawed, undiluted
1 teaspoon grated orange rind

2 cups heavy cream, whipped
12 double ladyfingers, split
2 oranges, peeled and sectioned
½ cup shredded coconut, toasted

Fold honey, orange juice and rind into whipped cream. Line bottom and sides of glass serving bowl with ladyfingers. Pour in orange cream and chill at least 4 hours or overnight. Decorate with fresh orange sections and toasted coconut sprinkled over the top.

Serves 8

LEMON ICE WITH RASPBERRY PURÉE

¾ cup sugar *or to taste*
¾ cup fresh lemon juice
Grated rind of 2 lemons
Dash salt
2 cups half-and-half

1 or 2 drops yellow food coloring
4 egg whites
¼ teaspoon cream of tartar
8 tablespoons sugar

For Lemon Ice: Place sugar in bowl and add lemon juice, lemon rind and salt; stir until sugar is dissolved. Pour in half-and-half and food coloring; mix well. Put in shallow container and freeze until mixture begins to solidify. Turn into food processor or blender and beat until light and frothy. Beat egg whites, adding cream of tartar when frothy. Add sugar by spoonfuls; continue beating until stiff peaks are formed and whites are glossy. Fold whites into partially frozen mixture and return to freezer. Freeze until mixture begins to solidify. Return to processor or blender and beat until light. Spoon back into the container. Freeze. Remove from freezer a few minutes before serving.

Raspberry Purée:

2 10½-ounce packages frozen
   raspberries, drained, reserve juice
½ of a 10½-ounce package frozen
   strawberries, drained, reserve juice

Additional sugar (optional)
1 tablespoon kirsch (optional)

For Raspberry Purée: Put raspberries and strawberries in blender or food processor and add about ¼ cup reserved fruit juice. Add additional sugar if desired. When proper consistency, blend in optional kirsch. Spoon over each serving of Lemon Ice.

Serves 8 to 10

LEMON ICE WITH RASPBERRY PURÉE — *"So good! Nice and light after a heavy meal."*

CRANBERRY UPSIDE DOWN CAKE
WITH CREME CHANTILLY

"Great holiday addition! For a change, try this easy, light cake made without the cranberries, baked in an angel food cake pan and topped with the tasty Lemon Sauce(page 83)."

4 cups fresh cranberries, picked
    over and washed
1⅓ cups sugar
1 cup egg whites (7 or 8 eggs)
½ teaspoon cream of tartar
2 cups all-purpose flour
1½ cups sugar
1 tablespoon baking powder

1 teaspoon salt
½ cup vegetable oil
5 egg yolks
¾ cup cold water
2 teaspoons vanilla
2 teaspoons grated lemon *or*
    orange rind

Preheat oven to 325°F. Grease and dust with sugar, 2 8-inch square baking pans. Evenly distribute 2 cups cranberries in bottom of each; evenly sprinkle ⅔ cup sugar over each. Tightly cover with foil and bake for 30 minutes; cool after removing foil.

In large bowl of mixer, beat egg whites and cream of tartar until soft peaks form. Set aside. Sift dry ingredients into large bowl. Add oil, yolks, water, vanilla and rind; beat until smooth. Fold in whites. Pour batter over cooled cranberries. Bake at 325°F for 30 minutes then increase to 350°F for 5 to 10 minutes. Let cakes sit for 10 minutes. Turn out onto cake racks to finish cooling. Prepare the following frosting:

Cream Chantilly: 2 tablespoons sugar
1 pint heavy cream   2 teaspoons vanilla extract

For Creme Chantilly: Beat cream, sugar and vanilla in a chilled bowl until soft peaks form. Frost cakes separately or join as one 2-layer cake. If desired use a pastry bag to pipe a few rosettes around the top and base of the cake(s).

Note: This cake does not need any adjustments for high altitude.

LEMON SAUCE

"Good served warm or cold . . ."

1 cup sugar	½ cup fresh lemon juice
2½ tablespoons cornstarch	1 tablespoon grated lemon rind
2 cups water	2 tablespoons butter or margarine
2 egg yolks, beaten	

Combine sugar and cornstarch in saucepan; gradually add water, blending until smooth. Cook over medium heat, stirring constantly until mixture becomes thick and clear; remove from heat. Stir small amount of hot mixture into egg yolks; add to hot mixture in saucepan and cook 2 minutes. Add lemon juice, rind and butter or margarine, blending well.

Makes 2¾ cups

WHITE ANGEL CAKE WITH ALMOND TOPPING

"A tasty approach to an iced angel food cake with a surprise topping . . ."

1 10-inch angel food cake

Frosting:	¼ cup light corn syrup
½ cup sugar	2 egg whites
2 tablespoons water	1 teaspoon vanilla

Mix sugar, water and corn syrup in saucepan. Cover saucepan; bring to rolling boil. Remove cover and cook to 242°F or until syrup spins a 6 to 8 inch thread. Just before syrup is ready, beat egg whites until stiff enough to hold a point. Pour hot syrup very slowly in a thin stream into beaten egg whites. Continue beating until frosting holds peaks. Blend in vanilla. Spread on cake, making pretty swirls with spatula.

Note: If mixing bowl of electric mixer is too narrow, beater will sling the sugar to sides of bowl (when pouring syrup into whites).

Altitude adjustment for syrup: For every 500 feet elevation over sea level, decrease end cooking point by 1 degree. For example, at 6000 feet, decrease the end cooking point by 12 degrees; hence your thermometer would read 230°F.

Almond Topping:	
3 tablespoons real butter	2 tablespoons half-and-half
1 cup confectioners' sugar	½ cup coarsely chopped toasted almonds

For Almond Topping: Melt butter in small skillet until quite brown, but be careful not to burn. Remove from heat and stir in confectioners' sugar and half-and-half. Stir in nuts. Topping should be consistency to drizzle. Add a bit more liquid if necessary. In a lacy design, drizzle frosting over top and down sides of frosted cake.

Serves 10

CARMEL-NUT APPLE PIE

"A beautiful and different approach to Continental Apple Pie."

10-inch double crust pastry
(see following)
¼ cup butter or margarine, softened
½ cup firmly packed brown sugar
2 tablespoons light corn syrup
½ cup pecan halves
5 large tart apples, pared, cored and
thinly sliced

1 tablespoon fresh lemon juice
½ cup sugar
1 tablespoon all-purpose flour
½ teaspoon ground cinnamon
½ teaspoon ground nutmeg
¼ teaspoon ground cloves

Prepare pie dough and refrigerate until ready to use. Grease a 10-inch pie plate liberally with 1 tablespoon butter or margarine. In small saucepan, melt remaining 3 tablespoons butter or margarine; add brown sugar and corn syrup; stir over heat only until dissolved, 1 to 2 minutes. Pour mixture in bottom of pie plate. Arrange pecan halves on plate in decorative design, rounded side down. Roll out lower crust; carefully fit over top of nut-sugar mixture. Trim crust even with outer edge of pie plate. Sprinkle apple slices with lemon juice. In bowl, combine sugar, flour and spices; toss with apple slices. Spread apple slices evenly in pie plate, peaking slightly in center. Roll out remaining pastry; place over apple mixture. Trim top crust ½ inch beyond edge of bottom crust; tuck it under edge of lower crust to seal. Flute edges. Cut slits in top crust. Bake in a preheated 400°F oven for 50 minutes. Remove from oven; cool 5 minutes. Place serving plate on top of pie, invert plate and carefully remove pie plate. Serve warm with a scoop of vanilla ice cream, if desired.

Serves 8

PASTRY FOR 10-INCH DOUBLE CRUST

2 cups sifted all-purpose flour
1 teaspoon salt

⅔ cup solid vegetable shortening
5 to 7 tablespoons cold water

Sift flour and salt together; cut in shortening with pastry blender until pieces are the size of small peas. (For extra-tender pastry, cut in half of shortening until like cornmeal. Cut in remaining until size of small peas.) Sprinkle 1 tablespoon water over part of mixture. Gently toss with fork; push to side of bowl. Repeat until all is moistened. Form into 2 balls. Flatten on lightly floured surface and refrigerate wrapped in foil until ready to use.

APRICOT REFRIGERATOR CAKE — "Light and simply delightful."

APRICOT REFRIGERATOR CAKE

1   10-inch angel food cake
1 tablespoon unflavored gelatin
¼ cup cold water
12 ounces dried apricots
1½ cups water
¾ cup sugar
1 cup water

1 teaspoon grated lemon rind
2 egg yolks, slightly beaten
⅛ teaspoon cream of tartar
2 egg whites, stiffly beaten
2 cups heavy cream, whipped
3 tablespoons confectioners' sugar

Soften gelatin in ¼ cup cold water. Cook apricots in 1½ cups water about 30 minutes. Reserve 6 apricots and purée remainder in blender or food processor. Put purée in saucepan with ¾ cup sugar, 1 cup water and lemon rind. Heat to boiling, stirring. Add some of the hot mixture to the egg yolks; return egg mixture to saucepan, stirring constantly; simmer 3 to 4 minutes. Remove from heat; add gelatin and stir until dissolved. Cool; chill until slightly thickened. Add cream of tartar to egg whites and beat until stiff peaks form; fold into apricot mixture. Slice cake horizontally in 4 to 5 layers. Spread mixture between layers and on top. Chill overnight. Frost with whipped cream to which the confectioners' sugar has been added. Decorate with reserved apricot halves, cut in strips.

Serves 10 to 12

SUNSHINE CAKE

"Want to know how to use those egg yolks that collect after making meringues, divinity, angel food cake and those good things? Here's the answer . . ."

¾ cup butter *or* margarine	¼ teaspoon salt
1¼ cups sugar	¾ cup milk
8 egg yolks	1 teaspoon vanilla
2½ cups all-purpose flour	1 teaspoon grated lemon rind
2½ teaspoons baking powder	

In large bowl of electric mixer, beat butter or margarine until creamy; add sugar gradually, continuing to beat until light. In separate bowl, beat egg yolks until light and lemon-colored; add to butter or margarine mixture and blend until just mixed. Sift together flour, baking powder and salt. Add alternately with milk to batter. Add vanilla and lemon rind. Bake in well-greased 9-inch tube pan in a preheated 350°F oven for about 45 minutes or until done when tested. Let cool 5 or 10 minutes then turn out onto serving plate. Prepare the following glaze.

Note: For high altitude, reduce baking powder to 2 teaspoons, increase milk by 1 tablespoon and increase flour by 2 tablespoons.

Orange Glaze:

1 cup confectioners' sugar	1 tablespoon melted butter
2 tablespoons orange juice	1½ teaspoons grated orange rind

For Orange Glaze: Place confectioners' sugar in small bowl and stir in other ingredients vigorously. Consistency should be thin enough to pour over top of cake. Drizzle over cake when it is cold.

Note: This cake should be eaten the day it is baked as it does not keep well.

STEAMED PLUM PUDDING

"The traditional Christmas dessert . . ."

1½ cups all-purpose flour	1½ cups dry bread crumbs
1 teaspoon baking soda	1 cup chopped nuts
1 teaspoon salt	1 cup finely ground suet
1 teaspoon ground cinnamon	1 cup chopped mixed candied fruit
½ teaspoon ground nutmeg	2 cups seedless raisins
½ teaspoon ground cloves	3 eggs, lightly beaten
¼ teaspoon ground ginger	⅓ cup dark molasses
⅔ cup firmly packed brown sugar	¾ cup milk

In a large mixing bowl, sift together flour, soda, salt, cinnamon, nutmeg, cloves and ginger; add brown sugar, bread crumbs, nuts, suet, candied fruit and raisins. Blend in eggs, molasses and milk. Pour batter into a well-greased 2-quart pudding mold and cover tightly. Or use any 2-quart mold, covered tightly and secured with string. Place the mold on a rack over 2 inches of boiling water in a large kettle. Cover kettle and steam pudding for 1½ hours or until the pudding springs back when touched with a finger and a tester inserted in the pudding comes out clean. Serve with Hard Sauce (page 75) or the following sauce.

Serves 12

LEMON SAUCE FOR STEAMED PLUM PUDDING

5 tablespoons sugar	2 cups boiling water
2 tablespoons all-purpose flour	Juice and grated rind of 1 lemon
1 tablespoon real butter	

Combine sugar and flour in saucepan over low heat; add butter. Gradually add 2 cups boiling water. Cook over medium heat, stirring until thick. Add juice and lemon rind and blend.

Makes 2 cups

GOODIES

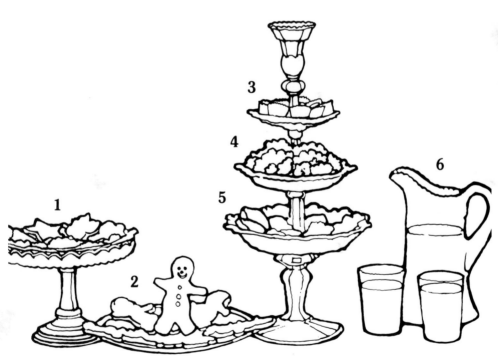

SUGAR COOKIES

"A good, simple, straight-forward sugar cookie . . ."

½ cup real butter	3 cups all-purpose flour
1 cup sugar	½ teaspoon salt
2 eggs	2 teaspoons baking powder
1 teaspoon vanilla	2 tablespoons milk

Cream butter and sugar together until light and fluffy. Add eggs, one at a time, beating well after each addition; stir in vanilla. Sift flour, salt and baking powder together; beat into creamed mixture alternately with milk. Form dough into flattened ball and wrap in foil; chill. Divide dough in fourths and roll on well-floured board to ⅛-inch thick; cut with various shaped cookie cutters. Place on greased baking sheet and bake in a preheated 350°F oven for 10 to 12 minutes or until lightly browned on outer edges. Remove to cake rack to cool. Decorate as desired.

Makes 4 to 6 dozen cookies, depending on size of cutters.

GINGER COOKIES

"Depending on thickness and on how long you bake these, you can have nice soft gingerbread cakes or crisp ginger cookies."

1 cup sugar	2 teaspoons each, ground ginger and
1 cup butter *or* margarine	cinnamon
2 eggs	2 teaspoons baking soda
1 cup light molasses	½ teaspoon salt
2 tablespoons cider vinegar	4½ cups all-purpose flour

Cream sugar and butter or margarine together, add eggs, beat well; add molasses and vinegar. Mix ginger, cinnamon, baking soda and salt into flour. Stir into creamed mixture, mixing well. Wrap dough in floured aluminum foil. Place in freezer for 1 hour. Remove; divide in fourths. Roll each piece of dough on well-floured board to ⅛-inch thick for plain cookies and ¼-inch thick for gingerbread men or other shapes. Bake in a preheated 350°F oven for 10 minutes. Remove to cake rack to cool. Repeat until all dough is used.

Note: If making gingerbread men, use currants for eyes, nose and mouth and red hot candies for buttons, or use following frosting for decorating.

Buttercream Frosting:	¼ cup water *or* milk
¼ cup butter *or* margarine	1 teaspoon vanilla *or* other flavoring
¼ cup solid vegetable shortening	1 pound confectioners' sugar

Beat all the above ingredients together until very smooth and creamy. You can tint portions of the frosting with food coloring according to your decorating scheme.

Makes approximately 3 dozen medium-size gingerbread men or more of smaller shapes.

Goodie

"*A delig*

1 cu
2 cu
4 ou
4 eg

Crea
to crea
pepper
dozen)
Sprinkl
using. V

Note
tiny pin

Makes

"*An eas*

In hea
wooden
Remove
fuls onto
Note:
by 1 deg
degrees;

Makes 1

OPERA FUDGE

1½ cups half-and-half	3 tablespoons real butter
3 tablespoons light corn syrup	1½ teaspoons vanilla
3 cups sugar	1 cup pecans, coarsely chopped
Pinch salt	

Butter heavy saucepan. Put half-and-half and corn syrup in pan and warm; stir in sugar and salt. Continue to stir over medium heat until dissolved. Put lid on pan for just a minute, then remove (this keeps sugar crystals from forming on side of pan). Cook over medium heat, without stirring, to 240° to 242°F on candy thermometer. Remove from heat immediately and pour out on marble slab or formica counter. Do not scrape saucepan; may cause fudge to crystalize. Put butter and vanilla in center and cool about 15 minutes or until edges are cool and center is lukewarm. Use a spatula to stir and knead candy until it loses its gloss, about 10 to 15 minutes. Quickly add nuts. Press fudge into a lightly greased 8-inch square pan. Cut into 1-inch squares.

Note: For every 500 feet elevation over sea level, decrease end cooking point by 1 degree. For example, at 6000 feet decrease the end cooking point by 12 degrees; hence your thermometer would read 228° to 230°F.

MERINGUE BARS

1 cup butter *or* margarine	½ teaspoon baking soda
½ cup firmly packed brown sugar	1 12-ounce package chocolate bits
½ cup granulated sugar	1 cup chopped nuts
4 egg yolks	4 egg whites
2 cups all-purpose flour	¼ teaspoon cream of tartar
1 teaspoon baking powder	½ cup confectioners' sugar

Cream butter or margarine, brown sugar and granulated sugar together, beating well. Add egg yolks, continuing to beat. Sift together flour, baking powder and soda; add to creamed mixture. Evenly spread into a well-greased 17x11-inch jelly roll pan. Sprinkle chocolate bits and nuts over mixture. Beat egg whites with cream of tartar; when soft peaks form, start adding confectioners' sugar a tablespoon at a time, beating well after each addition. Spread this over the batter in an even layer. Bake in a preheated 325°F oven for 35 minutes or until lightly browned. Remove from oven and score into 1½-inch squares while still warm. Cut into squares when cold.

Makes 4 dozen bars

OPERA FUDGE — "A smooth textured, elegant white fudge (top tier)." *DATE KISSES (middle tier)* — "These freeze well, retaining their golden color." *MERINGUE BARS* — "A chewy bar (bottom tier) with the rich flavor of chocolate bits."

DATE KISSES

2 egg whites	4 large shredded wheat biscuits,
½ cup sugar	rolled fine
1 cup quartered dates	1 teaspoon vanilla
1 cup chopped pecans	½ teaspoon salt

Beat egg whites until soft peaks form; add sugar gradually, beating until all sugar is added. Fold in remaining ingredients and drop by teaspoonfuls onto greased baking sheet. Bake in a preheated 350°F oven for 15 minutes. Remove from oven; let stand until cookies are set, about 10 to 15 minutes.

Makes 24 cookies

TRUFFETTES DU DAUPHINE

"Chocolate truffles so easy to make the children will enjoy helping you shape them . . ."

6 ounces semi-sweet chocolate	1 teaspoon liqueur (coffee *or* orange)
2 egg yolks	3 tablespoons real butter
2 tablespoons milk	Cocoa

Melt chocolate in double boiler; cool. Add egg yolks and mix thoroughly. Add milk and liqueur; continue to blend. Add butter, a few bits at a time, stirring well after each addition. Continue to beat until mixture is thoroughly blended. Cover and refrigerate 2 hours or longer, until mixture is firm. Shape into small ovals; roll in cocoa. Store in refrigerator or freezer.

Makes about 24 truffles

GOLDEN RUFFLE COOKIES

"For an added touch, place a single chocolate chip on top of each cookie just as they come out of the oven . . ."

2 egg whites	1 teaspoon vanilla
2 cups confectioners' sugar	2 cups toasted almonds *or* pecans
1 teaspoon white vinegar	broken into bits

Beat egg whites until stiff in medium-size bowl. Add sugar gradually, continuing to beat until stiff peaks form. Fold in remaining ingredients. Drop by teaspoonfuls onto greased baking sheet. Bake in a preheated 300°F oven for 15 minutes or until barely golden.

Makes about 24 cookies

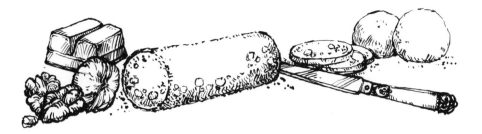

CHOCOLATE SNOW TOP COOKIES

"Everyone likes chocolate cookies, so here's another good one . . ."

2 ounces unsweetened chocolate
½ cup butter *or* margarine
1⅔ cups granulated sugar
2 teaspoons vanilla
2 eggs
2 cups all-purpose flour

2 teaspoons baking powder
½ teaspoon salt
⅓ cup milk
¾ cup chopped nuts
½ cup sifted confectioners' sugar

Melt chocolate in double boiler; cool. Thoroughly cream butter or margarine, sugar and vanilla together. Beat in eggs, then chocolate. Sift together dry ingredients; blend into egg and butter or margarine mixture alternately with milk. Add nuts. Chill 2 hours or longer. Form into 1-inch balls. Roll in confectioners' sugar. Place on greased baking sheets 2 to 3 inches apart. Bake in a preheated 350°F oven about 15 minutes or until done. Cool slightly, remove from pan to paper towels until cold. Should be stored in airtight tin.

Makes 4 dozen cookies

OATMEAL REFRIGERATOR COOKIES

"This is a favorite of my grandchildren."

1 cup firmly packed brown sugar
1 cup granulated sugar
1 cup butter *or* margarine
2 eggs
1½ cups all-purpose flour
½ teaspoon salt

1 teaspoon baking soda
1 teaspoon ground cinnamon
1 teaspoon ground nutmeg
1 cup chopped nuts
1 teaspoon vanilla
3 cups quick cooking oats

In large mixing bowl, cream sugars and butter or margarine together until light and fluffy. Beat in eggs one at a time. Sift together flour, salt, baking soda and spices. Mix nuts into sifted flour mixture and add to creamed mixture. Add vanilla. Stir in oats. Mixture will be rather stiff. Make into 2 rolls on wax paper and roll up; refrigerate overnight or for several days. Slice into thin slices and place on baking sheet. Bake in a preheated 350°F oven for 10 to 12 minutes or until done.

Makes about 6 to 7 dozen cookies

SNOWY ALMOND COOKIES

"A real taste treat."

⅔ cup butter *or* margarine	1 teaspoon vanilla
⅓ cup sugar	1 cup toasted almonds, coarsely
1⅓ cups all-purpose flour	chopped
⅛ teaspoon salt	Confectioners' sugar

Cream butter or margarine and sugar until light and fluffy. Add flour, salt, vanilla and almonds; work lightly with finger tips. Shape into small balls; place on greased baking sheet and flatten carefully with a dinner fork. Bake 25 minutes in a preheated 300°F oven. After they have cooled, roll in confectioners' sugar.

Makes about 4 dozen cookies

HOT CRANBERRY PUNCH

"The color of Christmas makes this punch appealing . . ."

1 pound fresh cranberries, washed and picked over	12 whole cloves
2 quarts water	4 cups orange juice
2 tablespoons grated orange rind	¼ to ½ cup fresh lemon juice
6 cinnamon sticks, about 2 inches long	1½ to 2 cups sugar

In a large saucepan combine cranberries, water, orange rind, cinnamon sticks and cloves. Cook until cranberries are soft; about 10 minutes. Strain. Add orange juice, lemon juice and sugar to cranberry juice. Heat until sugar is dissolved, stirring from time to time.

Note: Vary the lemon juice and sugar amounts according to desired tartness.

Makes 16 to 20 ½-cup servings

HOLIDAY WREATHS AND TREES

½ cup butter *or* margarine	15 to 20 drops green food coloring
30 large marshmallows	3½ cups corn flakes
1 teaspoon vanilla	⅓ cup red hot cinnamon candies

Melt butter or margarine and marshmallows together. Blend in vanilla and food coloring. Fold in corn flakes. Form into wreaths and Christmas trees on wax paper. Decorate with red hots.

Makes 3 dozen

HOLIDAY DELITE

*"A very good candy but expensive. Nice to give to your **best** friends. . . "*

3 cups sugar
1 cup white corn syrup
1½ cups half-and-half
¼ teaspoon salt
1½ teaspoons vanilla
½ pound Brazil nuts, sliced

½ pound pecan halves
½ pound broken walnuts
½ pound candied cherries, cut in half
½ pound candied pineapple, cut in
  small pieces

Combine sugar, corn syrup, half-and-half and salt in a heavy saucepan and boil to soft ball stage, 234° to 238°F. Remove from heat and start beating immediately. Add vanilla. When mixture thickens, add nuts and fruits, mixing well. Spread evenly in a well-greased 9x13-inch pan. When cool, cut into bite-size squares. This confection stores very well in a tightly covered container.

Note: For every 500 feet elevation over sea level, decrease end cooking point by 1 degree. For example, at 6000 feet decrease the end cooking point by 12 degrees; hence your thermometer would read 222° to 226°F.

Makes approximately 3½ pounds

HOLIDAY WREATHS AND TREES — "Children will love to help Mom with these."

HOLIDAY FRUIT COOKIES

1 cup pecans, chopped
1 cup candied cherries, chopped
1 cup pitted dates, chopped
¼ cup all-purpose flour
½ cup butter *or* margarine
1 cup firmly packed brown sugar
1 egg

2 teaspoons grated lemon rind
1½ cups all-purpose flour
½ teaspoon salt
½ teaspoon baking soda
¼ cup milk + 1 teaspoon cider
  vinegar; mix and let stand 10
  minutes

Combine pecans, cherries, dates and ¼ cup flour; mix lightly and set aside. Cream butter or margarine and brown sugar; add egg and lemon rind; mix well. Sift together 1½ cups flour, salt and baking soda; add to creamed mixture alternately with sour milk; blend well. Stir in fruit-nut mixture. Drop by teaspoonfuls onto greased baking sheet. Bake in a preheated 375°F oven for 10 to 12 minutes.

Makes 4 dozen cookies

TEA COOKIES IN TWO PARTS — "A rich, chewy, flavorful bar (shown upper right), so good with a cup of tea. APRICOT SQUARES — "These delightfully delicious little squares (center of round platter) are really rich, so the portions are cut small." HOLIDAY FRUIT COOKIES — (rim of round platter) "These will keep for a long time if kept out of sight!"

TEA COOKIES IN TWO PARTS

Part 1:
½ cup real butter

½ cup firmly packed brown sugar
1 cup all-purpose flour

Part 2:
2 eggs, beaten
¾ cup firmly packed
  brown sugar
1 teaspoon vanilla

1½ cups flaked coconut
2 tablespoons all-purpose flour
½ teaspoon baking powder
1 cup chopped walnuts

Grease a 9x13-inch baking pan. Combine all ingredients of part 1 and mix well. Press this into an even layer on bottom of baking pan. For part 2, beat eggs well; gradually add brown sugar and vanilla. Mix coconut, flour, baking powder and nuts; add to egg mixture. Mix well and carefully spoon and smooth over bottom layer. Bake in a preheated 350°F oven for 20 minutes. Let cool slightly; cut into squares.

Makes about 4 dozen squares

APRICOT SQUARES

1½ cups all-purpose flour
1 teaspoon baking powder
½ cup real butter, thinly sliced

1 egg, beaten
2 to 3 tablespoons milk
½ cup apricot preserves

Sift together flour and baking powder into medium-size bowl; cut in butter with pastry blender. Add beaten egg and milk; mix well. Press this dough into an even layer in a greased 8-inch square baking pan. Spread with apricot preserves.

Topping:
4 tablespoons real butter, melted
1 egg
1 cup sugar

1 cup flaked coconut
1½ cups chopped nuts
1 teaspoon vanilla

For topping: Mix melted butter with egg and sugar; beat well. Fold in coconut and nuts. Add vanilla and mix well. Spread this mixture over apricot layer. Bake in a preheated 350°F oven for 45 minutes. Cool and cut into 1-inch squares. Serve chilled.

Makes about 5 dozen squares

HOT FUDGE SAUCE

"Drizzle this sauce over ice cream or the unfrosted Sunshine Cake (page 86) . . ."

3 tablespoons real butter, cut into
   small pieces
⅓ cup granulated sugar
⅓ cup dark brown sugar, firmly
   packed

½ cup cocoa
⅓ cup half-and-half
Pinch salt

Place all ingredients in a heavy saucepan or double boiler. Stir over moderate heat until butter is melted. Reduce heat; continue to stir and scrape bottom and sides of pan with rubber spatula until sugar is melted. Bring sauce to boiling point; do not boil. Serve warm or hot.

Note: May be kept in refrigerator in covered jar. Reheat slowly in top of double boiler before serving. If it becomes too thick, thin with a little milk.

Makes 1 cup sauce

FESTIVE CARAMEL POPCORN AND NUTS

"Have a friend stir the corn and nuts while you pour the cooked caramel syrup. This way you can evenly distribute the caramel while pouring. . . ."

3 quarts white popped corn
1 cup pecan halves
¼ cup whole almonds
1½ cups sugar

1 cup real butter
½ cup light corn syrup
¼ teaspoon salt
1 teaspoon vanilla

Mix popped corn and nuts on a greased jelly roll pan. Combine sugar, butter, corn syrup and salt in a 2-quart pan and bring to boil over medium heat, stirring constantly. Continue to boil, stirring constantly for 15 minutes or until "caramel colored." Remove pan from heat and stir in vanilla. Pour this mixture over popped corn and nuts and immediately begin to mix. When cold, break into pieces to store.

CANDIED CRANBERRIES

"A beautiful, glossy red accompaniment to any dish . . ."

2 cups raw cranberries, picked over and washed
1 cup sugar

Spread cranberries in an even layer in a shallow baking dish. Sprinkle berries with sugar and cover dish securely with foil. Bake in a preheated 350°F oven for one hour, stirring occasionally. Chill cranberries and serve with poultry or pork, as a condiment.

Note: This may be made ahead and frozen to use as desired.

Makes 2 cups

MENUS

CHRISTMAS EVE PARTY
Serves 8

Oxtail Soup in Mugs

Chicken in the Snow

Broccoli Spears with Lemon Butter

Dinner Muffins

Date-Nut Pudding

NEW YEAR'S EVE PARTY
Serves 8

Tuna Paté

Corn, Cheese, Chili Pie

Green Salad

Rainbow Bombe

OR

Tuna Paté

Party Goulash

Buttered Rice or Noodles

Green Salad

Rainbow Bombe

OXTAIL SOUP IN MUGS

"This is a heartwarming and palate-tingling first course to serve in mugs while everyone is standing 'round the tree . . ."

2 2⅝-ounce packages imported oxtail soup mix
8 cups cold water

½ cup dry sherry *or* dry marsola wine
½ cup dairy sour cream
¼ cup minced fresh parsley

Pour soup mix into saucepan and add 8 cups cold water, stirring to mix well. Bring to boil, stirring constantly. Reduce heat, partially cover saucepan and allow to simmer for 10 minutes. Stir in wine and sour cream and bring just to boil, stirring. Pour into heated mugs and sprinkle top with minced parsley before serving.

CHICKEN IN THE SNOW

6 cups chicken broth (your own *or* canned)
2 celery ribs, cut in 2-inch segments
1 large onion, studded with 1 clove
1 large carrot, pared and cut in 2-inch segments
1 lemon slice
½ teaspoon salt
8 to 10 fresh parsley stems, ½ bay leaf, ½ teaspoon dried thyme tied in cheesecloth
3½ pounds chicken breasts, skinned, boned and cut in 1½-inch squares

5 tablespoons real butter
¼ cup all-purpose flour
2 tablespoons fresh lemon juice
Freshly ground white pepper
3 egg yolks
1 cup heavy cream
24 medium fresh mushroom caps
2 tablespoons real butter
1 10½-ounce package frozen peas, cooked
Salt and freshly ground pepper to taste

In large saucepan, put chicken broth, celery, onion with clove, carrot, lemon slice and salt. Bring to boil; add herbs tied in cheesecloth, lower heat and simmer 45 minutes. Add chicken pieces and gently simmer for 7 to 10 minutes. Remove chicken and set aside. Strain broth and reserve. In saucepan, melt 5 tablespoons butter and add flour; stir for 3 to 4 minutes. Add reserved broth and bring to boil; simmer over medium heat for 20 to 25 minutes or until reduced to 4 cups. Stir lemon juice and white pepper into sauce. In small bowl, mix egg yolks and heavy cream together until well blended. Blend some hot sauce into egg mixture then return to sauce; cook over low heat, stirring until sauce thickens. Do not boil.

Sauté mushroom caps in 2 tablespoons butter for 5 to 6 minutes; sprinkle very lightly with salt and pepper. Add mushroom caps and peas to sauce. Add chicken pieces.* Return sauce almost to boiling point. Add salt and pepper to taste. Serve chicken in chafing dish with rice in a separate bowl. Garnish rice with tomato wedges if desired.

*Note: If making ahead, stop here. Cool and refrigerate. Before serving, slowly bring to boiling point in a preheated 350°F oven, about 30 minutes.

BROCCOLI SPEARS WITH LEMON BUTTER

3 10½-ounce packages frozen
   broccoli spears
½ cup real butter

2 tablespoons fresh lemon juice
Few drops Tabasco® pepper sauce

Cook broccoli spears according to package directions and drain well. Return to saucepan to keep hot. In small saucepan, melt butter; add lemon juice and Tabasco® pepper sauce to taste; bring to boil. Immediately remove from heat and pour over broccoli spears.

DINNER MUFFINS

1½ cups all-purpose flour
½ cup sugar
1½ teaspoons baking powder
½ teaspoon salt

¼ cup butter *or* margarine, melted
½ cup milk
2 eggs

In bowl, mix together flour, sugar, baking powder and salt. Add butter or margarine, milk and eggs. Beat until all ingredients are just moistened. Grease a 12-cup muffin pan and fill ⅔ full with batter. Bake for 15 to 18 minutes in a preheated 400°F oven.

Makes 12 muffins

DATE-NUT PUDDING

6 eggs, separated	1½ cups pitted dates, chopped
1 cup sugar	1 cup English walnuts, broken
⅔ cup fine saltine cracker crumbs	1 cup heavy cream
1 tablespoon baking powder	2 tablespoons sugar

Beat egg whites until stiff, but not dry; set aside. Beat egg yolks; add sugar and beat well. Mix in cracker crumbs, baking powder, dates and walnuts. Fold in egg whites. Bake in greased 8-inch square pan in a preheated 375°F oven for 45 minutes. Beat cream with sugar until soft peaks form. Cut pudding into squares and serve with a dollop of sweetened whipped cream.

TUNA PATÉ

1 7-ounce can tuna with oil	3 tablespoons unsalted, shelled pistachio nuts
2 to 3 tablespoons brandy	
2 3-ounce packages low-calorie cream cheese	1 10½-ounce can beef consommé (with gelatin) chilled until almost jelled
2 hard-cooked eggs	
1 teaspoon fresh lemon juice	Lemon slices
Salt and freshly ground white pepper to taste	Fresh parsley sprigs

Place tuna, oil and brandy in food processor or blender and process until tuna is well broken up. Add remaining ingredients (except consommé, lemon slices and parsley), one at a time, processing until each is well mixed. Spoon mixture into 3-cup greased mold. Smooth the surface. Spread with partially jelled consommé and refrigerate until firm. Unmold. Garnish with lemon slices and parsley sprigs. Serve with crackers or raw vegetable sticks.

CORN, CHEESE AND CHILI PIE

3 eggs	1 cup dairy sour cream
1 1-pound can creamed corn	4 ounces Monterey Jack cheese, cut in ½-inch cubes
1 10½-ounce package frozen corn, thawed and drained	
½ cup butter *or* margarine, melted	1 4-ounce can diced green chilies
½ cup yellow cornmeal	½ teaspoon salt
	½ teaspoon Worcestershire sauce

Beat eggs in large mixing bowl. Add all remaining ingredients and stir until thoroughly blended. Grease 2 9-inch round pie pans or 1 shallow oven casserole; pour in mixture and bake in a preheated 350°F oven for 50 to 60 minutes, depending on size of pan. Pie should be firm to touch in center and golden on top.

Note: May be frozen before baking; bring to room temperature before baking. Pie will keep in refrigerator for 2 to 3 days before cooking.

PARTY GOULASH

4 pounds boneless beef chuck,
  trimmed, cut into bite-size pieces
½ cup all-purpose flour
½ cup vegetable oil
2 cloves garlic, minced
2 tablespoons paprika
2 teaspoons salt
½ teaspoon freshly ground pepper
  or to taste

2 bay leaves
¼ cup tomato paste
2 10½-ounce cans beef broth
2 cups each thickly sliced onion,
  celery, green pepper and carrots
1 cup dairy sour cream
⅓ cup minced fresh parsley

Sprinkle cubed beef with flour. Heat vegetable oil in Dutch oven until very hot; brown meat ½ pound at a time, removing browned pieces to a dish. When browning is complete, return meat to Dutch oven; add garlic, paprika, salt, pepper, bay leaves, tomato paste and beef broth. Bring to boil and stir well. Cover and place in preheated 350°F oven and cook for 1½ to 2 hours or until meat is tender. For last hour of cooking time, add sliced vegetables; continue cooking. Just before removing from oven, stir in sour cream and taste for seasoning; heat through. Serve over wide noodles or rice with a sprinkling of minced parsley.

RAINBOW BOMBE

"Refreshing and a delight to behold . . ."

2 quarts orange sherbet	1 quart raspberry sherbet
¼ cup Curaçao	2 tablespoons kirsch
2½ tablespoons grated orange rind	1 pint lemon sherbet
1 teaspoon grated lemon rind	2 to 3 tablespoons white creme de menthe

Soften orange sherbet to room temperature; beat in Curaçao, orange and lemon rinds. Spoon sherbet into a large chilled mold to within 4 inches of top. Freeze. When orange sherbet is hard, spread a 2-inch layer of softened raspberry sherbet beaten with kirsch over orange sherbet leaving space for lemon sherbet. Freeze again. When raspberry sherbet is hard, fill remaining layer with lemon sherbet beaten with creme de menthe. Smooth top of mold and cover with foil. Refreeze.

Note: To serve, remove from freezer and dip into hot water for a second; unmold onto a serving dish and slice to serve. Return remaining servings to freezer for another time.

MENUS

CHILDREN'S TREE TRIMMING PARTY
Serves 8

Hot Spiced Apple Juice

Sloppy Joes

OR

Hot Tuna Buns

Heavenly Hash

CHRISTMAS DAY FAMILY BRUNCH
Serves 8

Scandinavian Fruit Soup

Great Big Pancake

Homemade Pork Sausage

Pineapple-Nut Cookies

HOT SPICED APPLE JUICE

8 very small apples
2 tablespoons butter *or* margarine,
  melted
⅓ cup granulated sugar
2 quarts apple juice or cider

½ cup firmly packed brown sugar
2 whole nutmegs
4 cinnamon sticks
16 whole cloves
16 whole allspice

Core apples and remove skin from top ⅓ of each apple, or quarter and core each apple. Place in baking pan. Brush with butter or margarine; sprinkle with granulated sugar. Roast in a preheated 350°F oven 30 to 45 minutes until tender. Baking time will depend on size and variety of apple. In large saucepan, combine apple juice or cider and brown sugar. Tie spices in cheesecloth bag; crush with hammer or mallet and add to saucepan. Bring to boil, cover, reduce heat and simmer 15 minutes. Remove spice bag; discard.

To serve, pour hot spiced apple juice into tureen or punch bowl. Float hot, roasted apples on surface. Ladle into mugs and top each serving with a roasted apple. If desired, leave apples in bowl until cider is finished. Place in dish to be eaten like a dessert, maybe with a scoop of vanilla ice cream.

SLOPPY JOES

3 pounds lean ground beef
2 medium onions, chopped
¾ cup chopped celery
1 6-ounce can tomato paste
2 8-ounce cans tomato sauce
¾ cup water
2 teaspoons salt

1 tablespoon chili powder
2 tablespoons Worcestershire sauce
Several dashes Tabasco® pepper
  sauce
3 tablespoons cider vinegar
¼ cup sugar
8 hamburger buns

In large skillet, brown hamburger with onions and celery. Add next 9 ingredients and simmer for 1 hour, stirring occasionally. Serve meat over buns.

Note: Leftovers may be used to serve another time.

HOT TUNA BUNS

2 7-ounce cans Albacore tuna,
   drained
1 cup diced Cheddar cheese
½ cup sliced stuffed green olives

4 green scallions, sliced
½ cup real mayonnaise
1 tablespoon tomato paste
8 poppyseed hamburger buns

Flake tuna and combine first 6 ingredients. Fill buns and wrap in aluminum foil. Bake in a preheated 350°F oven for 15 to 20 minutes. Serve in foil to keep good and hot.

Note: These freeze well. Bring to room temperature before baking.

HEAVENLY HASH

"The children will love this combination and so will everyone else . . ."

1 3-ounce package strawberry-
   flavored gelatin
1 3-ounce package lemon-flavored
   gelatin

1 cup heavy cream, whipped
1 cup miniature marshmallows
2 large bananas, sliced
1 cup flaked coconut

Prepare gelatins according to package instructions and pour each flavor into an 8-inch square pan to set. When set cut into 1-inch cubes. Whip cream in large bowl and fold in marshmallows and sliced bananas, fold in cubes of gelatin and coconut. Chill until serving time.

SCANDINAVIAN FRUIT SOUP

¾ cup pitted prunes
¾ cup dried apricots
6 cups cold water
1 cup sugar
¼ cup quick-cooking tapioca
3 lemon slices, ¼-inch thick

1 stick cinnamon, about 2 inches
   long
1 cup peeled, diced apples
¼ cup raisins
¼ cup currants

In medium-size saucepan, soak prunes and apricots in 6 cups water for 30 minutes. Add sugar, tapioca, lemon slices and cinnamon stick; bring to boil and simmer for 10 minutes. Add apples, raisins and currants. Simmer for 10 minutes more.

GREAT BIG PANCAKE

6 eggs
1 cup all-purpose flour
1 teaspoon salt
1 cup milk

¼ cup butter *or* margarine, melted
Whipped cream
Strawberries
Maple syrup

Beat eggs with whisk or electric mixer until well blended. Sift together flour and salt; add slowly to eggs, beating until smooth. Add milk and butter or margarine. Generously grease bottom and sides of unheated 8½ or 9-inch skillet and pour in half the batter. Bake in preheated 450°F oven for 20 minutes, reduce heat to 350°F and bake an additional 5 to 10 minutes. Do not open oven until last 5 minutes of baking time. Serve immediately with whipped cream and strawberries, maple syrup or fruit and syrup of your choice.

Note: If you have 2 skillets, bake 2 pancakes at once. Have another batter ready to put 2 more in the oven when the first ones come out, for a hungry crowd.

HOMEMADE PORK SAUSAGE

2 pounds lean pork, cut into 1-inch
squares
1 pound pork fat, cut into 1-inch
squares
¼ teaspoon cayenne pepper

2 tablespoons dried sage, crumbled
or 2 teaspoons rubbed sage
1 teaspoon salt
¼ teaspoon freshly ground pepper

Use medium blade on meat grinder or steel blade with food processor and grind pork coarsely. Add rest of ingredients and grind or blend again. Do not process too fine. Shape into patties and sauté over low heat until browned on both sides and cooked through.

PINEAPPLE-NUT COOKIES

½ cup butter *or* margarine
½ cup firmly packed brown sugar
½ cup granulated sugar
1 egg
1 8-ounce can crushed pineapple,
well drained

¼ teaspoon baking powder
¼ teaspoon baking soda
¼ teaspoon salt
2 cups unbleached flour
1 teaspoon vanilla
½ cup slivered, toasted almonds

Cream butter or margarine with sugars. Add egg and pineapple and mix well.
Mix together baking powder, baking soda and salt with flour; add to pineapple mixture. Mix well; add vanilla. Fold in nuts. Drop batter by teaspoonfuls onto greased cookie sheet and bake in a preheated 350°F oven for 10 to 12 minutes.

Note: These are good frosted. Use powdered sugar and enough pineapple juice to moisten to spreading consistency.

Recipe Index

Born and raised in Topeka, Kansas, **MIRIAM BAKER LOO** is an accomplished and creative homemaker who has been an enthusiastic cook since her youth. After graduation from Washburn University of Topeka, Kansas, she was married to Orin Loo. In addition to raising three sons, with her husband, in 1950 she founded Current, Inc., a national mail order firm located in Colorado Springs. The company has grown from a basement business, whose first product lines included Post-A-Notes and recipe cards designed by Mr. Loo, to a thriving enterprise serving millions of customers today.

A participant in many goumet food classes, Miriam Loo has been responsible for the many recipes for notes, calendars and personal enclosures in the Current product line for several years.

Long involved in volunteer activities, Miriam Loo has received national recognition for her accomplishments in community work, church leadership and business.

The decorative holiday house on the front cover of the Holiday Cookbook was constructed by Current artists, who used Baker's Clay for the basic structure. To make your own smaller Christmas decorations of this material, mix together 2 cups flour, ½ cup salt, and ¾ to 1 cup water. Knead for 5 minutes until clay-like and form decorations. Bake for 1½ hours at 350°F or air dry overnight. Paint and varnish when dried.